BOMBPROOF

BOMB PROOF

A Field Proven Guide
for the
New-to-Role Executive

————

EMILY BERMES

To my dear friend Erin Correa who hired
to me to tackle the problem of executives' "failure
to assimilate" in the first place. I would never have
learned any of this, if not for your faith in me to fix it.
Thanks friend, for changing my life.

To my amazing husband, who is supportive beyond
reason, loving beyond measure, and shows his
dedication to our family every single day. You, my
friend are the best thing that has *ever* happened to me.

And to my writing partner Jon Anderson.
Thank you for the structure, encouragement,
support, laughter, and occasional harassment.
This book would <u>not</u> exist without you.

Bombproof: A Field Proven Guide for the New-to-Role Executive by Emily Bermes

Cover by Faceout Studio

ISBN: 978-1-7369420-0-0 (paperback)
ISBN: 978-1-7369420-1-7 (ebook)
ISBN: 978-1-7369420-2-4 (hardback)

First Edition September 2021

Printed in the United States of America

More information available at bebombproof.com

Ordering information: Special discounts are available for quantity orders for corporations, associations, and others. For more information, contact ebermes@ bermesassociates.com

Want to join the conversation? Use #bebombproof on social media channels.

TABLE OF
CONTENTS

BOMBPROOF TESTIMONIALS

"Great advice based on real-world examples. A must read for anyone that wishes to be successful in a new executive role by learning from experiences of others!"

SONJA COX
Chief Executive Ofiicer
Southern Maryland Electric Cooperative

"The partnership, thought leadership, and wisdom that Emily brings is second to none. She's always looking around the next corner to unlock value for the people that she partners with. This book could not be more on-point with the evolving challenges of executive onboarding. This is a must-read and provides game-changing insights."

MICHAEL PULCANIO
Chief Human Resource Officer
Schwans

"Emily's work with our leadership team has had a terrific impact on every team member she has worked with. Her instinctive ability to learn an organization's culture and leverage it with her engagements has helped us to smartly evolve the business."

DAVID M FINDLAY
President and Chief Executive Officer
Lake City Bank

"The information you receive from Emily Bermes + Associates is second to none. It provides perspective and gives you the tools to drive your personal performance in a way that generates significant business value. An incredible tool for any senior leader in today's business world."

PETER ILLIAN
Senior Vice President
Discover Financial Services

"Emily's insights helped me to navigate a new Officer level role that was not only 'not as expected' but far, far more challenging than expected. With her support and expertise, not only was I successful (and happy) in my new role, but my seamless assimilation also led to a fast string of promotions which were easier to adapt to with the framework she taught me. The framework absolutely works, no matter the size of the organization or the complexity of the charter."

ARIJIT ROY
Executive Vice President
Retail Bank

"Given how critical the first few months are in a new role, it's amazing how little literature and attention is focused on executive onboarding. It's no wonder so many leaders struggle when new leaders are promoted into new roles. Coaching from Emily during my on-boarding has been priceless because it bridged the gap between I thought I needed to do, and what was actually needed to be successful. We all think we have that awareness, but given failure rates it's clear that we don't - and coaching is an underutilized tool in new role assimilation."

DAVID NATHAN
Director of Treasury & Risk Management
Fox Factory

Foreword

FOREWORD

Over 20 years into my professional career, and this was the first time I'd ever had a "coach."

To this point, I had been able to wander through the initial stages of new positions and figure things out over time. But this new position I was being promoted into was different. I was going to be responsible for a huge piece of the business, hundreds of employees, and a much wider scope, including multiple functions where I didn't have years of experience to help guide me.

That promotion is how I found myself looking out my office window one day, phone up to my ear as Emily told me to close my eyes and take a few deep breaths.

"What kind of voodoo is this?" I thought to myself, but I decided to lean into it and do what she was asking. What I didn't realize at the time was that Emily inherently understood the issues I was facing, even if she wasn't in the day-to-day of the business. And she was able to overlay that understanding with her frameworks, allowing me to view my situation from multiple vantage points and ultimately, create meaningful engagements with my partners to help drive the business, the team, and myself forward.

"You got this!" was the common refrain that Emily would leave me with at the end of each of our coaching sessions.

As you read this book, you will learn about three critical areas that determine an executive's success as they take on a new role. Those three areas will seem straightforward and practical, but I'm still struck to this day by the fact that they aren't taught, and by how many people struggle in new roles as a result. Finish this book and you will be able to develop practical implementations of what Emily teaches, including understanding:

- What your job actually is – not just from your boss' view, but from the viewpoint of all of the key stakeholders, including your team, peers, other departments, and, of course, your boss.
- How you can get things done – the best strategies for the culture of the organization, so you can create positive engagements as you work to deliver your business goals.
- Where your team is at – what the people most critical to your success need from you to achieve their best.

It won't be the same as having Emily on the phone giving you positive reinforcement on a weekly basis, but if you embrace these lessons, you likely won't need as much of that as I did.

Good luck on your journey – you got this!

And to Emily, thank you again for playing an important role in my development, and for helping me to create the success that I've been fortunate enough to generate in my career.

Peter Illian, SVP Discover Financial Services

Roy

Roy

"What the hell did I get myself into?"

Roy was looking directly at us. He'd asked the question in obvious frustration, but there was also legitimate curiosity written on his face. My coworker and I sat across from him at a table in the corner of a vast corporate cafeteria, trying to remain anonymous against the backdrop of the steady lunchtime buzz. Around us, the company's employees greeted each other, laughing and carrying on the kind of familiar business conversations that make workdays feel normal. At our table, though, we were trying to keep our voices down. At least, we *had* been trying.

Roy was getting animated, and it was hard to blame him.

THE PROBLEM

I was meeting with Roy because he had recently taken on a VP position, running a business unit at a Fortune 500 financial services firm. He'd been handpicked for the role and his selection was entirely warranted.

Roy was whip-smart.

He'd immigrated to the States, alone, when he was barely more than a kid. He was determined to make something of himself and earn his family's pride. By any outside estimation, he'd succeeded marvelously.

He'd put himself through college by working at a pizza place, gone on to get an MBA at Harvard, then followed that up by taking a lucrative position at McKinsey. From there, he'd worked his way up in a fiercely competitive environment on the basis of consistently great work. Soon, he found himself in a position to be poached by a big corporation for a very visible role.

When he got the offer, he was delighted, of course. On paper, taking a VP role at this company seemed like a dream come true. He was more than qualified. The role would be the next step in his string of successes and a fitting reward for all of his hard work.

But in practice, it was becoming clear that the role was less of a dream and closer to a nightmare.

"What the hell did I get myself into?" he asked us again, his words cutting uncomfortably clearly through the clatter of conversations at nearby tables. My coworker and I shifted awkwardly in our seats. "I mean, really," he said more loudly, "how is it even possible for a place to be so [messed] up?"

I've heard that exact line too many times, and I've never found a good answer to the question.

Maybe this goes without saying, but I was nervous.

I'd been working with Roy's new employer for years through a series of executive coaching engagements. Overall, my experience with the company had been a good one: challenging but fulfilling, with all of my clients making measurable improvements that satisfied their direct managers. Before Roy, though, all of my work had been focused on established executives, the kind of leaders in big organizations who have existing relationships and a few (hopefully correctable) recurring weaknesses. I'd never worked with someone so fresh to their seat.

And I'd never worked with a seat that was so clearly on fire.

Roy's role had been pitched to him as a turn-around project for an underperforming business unit. He'd taken the job expecting a challenge; what he found upon arrival was a hopeless case. His charter, he was coming to understand, required him to salvage a sinking ship in a short amount of time with a team that was already underwater.

The unit's performance had been in decline for four years, and during that time, three predecessors to Roy had been hired and tasked with reversing course. Each one had failed hard and left fast. The constant state of leadership flux, coupled with the unit's steady decline in performance, had left Roy's new team dejected and embittered.

Things had gotten to the point that the group were openly hostile to any suggestion of change. In fact, as I interviewed the unit's team members to size up the situation, the core messages I heard again and again were:

"Screw this."

"I can't get behind one more hotshot's good ideas."

"I'm done."

There wasn't much good to glean and there was no getting around the obvious: This was an intimidating assignment. And it was probably destined to fail. And I *hate* to fail.

"What the hell have *we* gotten ourselves into?"
I began to ask myself. After all, I had a stake in
Roy's success, too.

So as Roy sat across the table from us, frustration in his voice and worry in his eyes, I didn't
have an answer to his questions or much confidence in our combined ability to make his role
work.

But we both knew that we had to try. It was too
late to back out.

We both were now on the hook for this
turnaround.

THE PLAN

While I didn't have answers for Roy, I did have a
question.

"How long do you have to make things work?"
I asked. "Six months? Two years? What are we
working with?"

Roy didn't know.

As I've found out since, this is a common occurrence; many new executives take roles without an explicit understanding of how long they have to fulfill their charters. There may be an implicit assumption—in our case, for example, Roy and I knew that the situation was urgent, but we both lacked specifics. It's hard to build a good strategy that is based on assumptions. If we only had six months, for example, we didn't want to chart out a yearlong roadmap. But if we had two years, we didn't need to pour fuel on the fire with a manufactured sense of urgency.

So the first thing we did was clarify with Roy's boss exactly how long he had to turn things around. As it turned out, he had 15 months. Given the state of the unit, a turnaround in that timeframe seemed unlikely, but the knowledge was a start. Armed with it, we set to work.

There was some expectation that in order for Roy to implement a turnaround, he would have to clean house and refresh his team's talent. Based on our 15-month timeframe and the difficulty of talent acquisition in this industry, we didn't have time to do that. Unfortunately, we also didn't believe we had time to turn things around with the existing team. Our analysis of the situation had revealed that Roy's team, despite having incredibly low morale, was actually fairly talented. But it had also shown that they were obviously entrenched in a terrible culture left by a string of failed leaders. Changing the status quo quickly seemed unlikely.

Caught between a rock and a hard place, we went with Roy's gut: He believed his people could do good work if they had the chance. "I'd rather take heat from my boss and delay expectations," he said, "than fire talented people."

With that approach as the starting point, Roy and I developed a seven-pronged plan that we felt gave us the best chance of turning things around. Here's what it included:

1. **STRENGTHENING THE TEAM THROUGH THE PROMOTION OF TALENT AS APPROPRIATE.**

We wanted to start by equipping and encouraging people. We also imported talent to augment this approach, but the core of our work was focused on existing personnel.

2. **CREATING RIGOR IN PROCESS-ORIENTED THINKING THROUGH DISCIPLINE, ROLE CLARITY, AND DATA-DRIVEN DECISION MAKING.**

This included a review of all complaints and incident data to ensure situations were properly addressed.

3. **STAYING TRUE TO PRIORITIES AND KEEPING FOCUS ON THE CUSTOMER.**

In the midst of change—and in the wake of leadership flux—there was too much going on. We knew we needed to make customers' needs our North Star.

REPAIRING RELATIONSHIPS WITH FIELD AND MARKETING TEAMS BY PERSONALLY VISITING WITH LEADERS.

Roy's predecessors had burned a few bridges. So he went to his peers and worked to rebuild them by developing a shared sense of purpose. Our hope was that with alignment, collaboration would become possible for his own direct reports.

⑤ CUTTING 30 OF THE 70 ACTIVE INITIATIVES HIS TEAM HAD BEEN WORKING ON.

This was huge. Roy's predecessors had identified plenty of problems, but the team simply wasn't in a place to effectively address all of them. Out of the 70 initiatives that were active when Roy accepted the role, most of them were superfluous. He chose to focus on 40. The idea was that, by making people's lives easier, we'd slowly make real progress toward what mattered most.

(6) REORGANIZING THE UNIT TO PROVIDE A MORE LOGICAL STRUCTURE THAT ALIGNED WITH THE CUSTOMER LIFECYCLE.

Again, the unit had been in disarray. Getting a solid foundation was necessary before his team could generate better results.

(7) FILLING CRITICAL ROLES QUICKLY.

With the new structure outlined, there were some essential seats that needed to be filled. We promoted talented internal team members and brought in talent where it was needed. Our goal was to promote clearly defined roles that would result in an abundance of ownership.

This process was not a quick fix. It involved intensive planning and it took time.

But, to our surprise, it didn't take 15 months.

THE RESULTS

A year after I'd first met Roy in a crowded cafeteria, he was no longer asking unanswerable questions. Now, when we sat in that crowded cafeteria, I didn't worry that his people would overhear depressing details about their leadership.

Against all odds, Roy was having a blast.

The change had been incredible. The time Roy had taken to listen to issues, the busywork he'd gotten rid of, the collaboration and trust he'd built—it had all paid off to steadily raise team morale out of the depths.

The progress didn't happen overnight, but as Roy remained consistent over several months, the bitterness and dejection that had hung like clouds over his team gradually dissipated. And as the mood within the unit had improved, so had its performance.

It turns out Roy had been right: His team was talented.

Because he'd slowed down and taken care of them, they'd been able to perform. In fact, they performed so well that they went on to win a JD Power and Associates Second Place Award just two years after Roy was hired.

Honestly, I was stunned. I was also hooked on helping executives with their assimilation strategy. Big time.

On the basis of a sound executive strategy and patient execution, Roy had taken a turnaround project and turned it into a triumph. This was incredibly fulfilling, and I knew that there were lessons in it. I wanted to codify them and bring them to other new-to-role executives.

I believed this could be game-changing.

Because the more I delved into the hard work of executive assimilation, the more I became convinced of a hard truth: Most people's experiences are nothing like Roy's.

Fifty Percent of New-to-Role Executives Fail

Fifty Percent of New-to-Role Executives Fail

If you take an executive role, you have roughly a 50% chance of failing within 18 months.

Executive failure is far too costly for it to happen so frequently. I'll get into the data behind this soon, but first, take a moment to let the weight of the statistic hit you. Given the stakes involved in executive roles and the assumed intelligence of the people like you who are considered for them, a 50% failure rate is ... ridiculous.

Questions naturally follow: Why do the people like you—who are supposedly the smartest in the room—fail half of the time they move into a new seat? Why do board members and executives and

organizations have a coin-flip chance of successfully hiring leaders for their most important roles?

Those are good lines of inquiry, and I'll use most
of this book to unpack and answer those two
questions. For now, I'd like to return the focus to
the problem itself so that you understand it as
clearly as possible.

What does failure mean? How often does it happen?
And what does it cost?

THE DEFINITION OF EXECUTIVE FAILURE

First, let's define what is meant by the word 'failure'—and yes, unfortunately, it *is* about as bad as
it sounds.

Nearly all research on executive failure defines
it as attrition without accomplishment. In other
words, executives who fail leave their roles
within 18 months of taking them and they
leave for some reason other than that they've

accomplished their objectives. They're gone before results are achieved.

There are three main ways that failure happens:

The First Way To Fail Is To Be Fired

It might comfort you to know that it's rare that an executive is fired before 18 months is up. Still, it does happen. Typically, it requires either gross incompetence on the part of the executive or some kind of incontrovertible and public moral failing. Don't worry: This only happens about 3% of the time[1]. If you are not committing fraud or assault, you probably won't be fired. (Pro tip: Don't do those things.)

The Second Way to Fail Is to Quit

Quitting is rare, too. But sometimes, the role is so painful that executives choose to simply drop it, exit the organization, and get away. If this happens, it's almost certainly due to a huge

---

1   https://www.businessinsider.com/reasons-executives-fail-2015-3

misunderstanding or misalignment of expectations. Do a basic level of research before you take a role and, assuming the organization isn't nefariously keeping things from you, you can probably avoid having to quit before 18 months is up.

The Third Way to Fail is to Flail

This path is the most common of the three, and it's the one you'll find most difficult to guard against if you don't understand how to prepare for your new role. Executives who flail usually (unknowingly) make some costly early missteps that isolate them from power and the ability to influence others. Over time, these mistakes increasingly diminish their ability to perform in the role. They quietly and ineffectively struggle against gravity until they are eventually displaced—either by taking a role elsewhere or by being forcibly reassigned.

It's not fun. But it's not uncommon. If you are fired, quit, or flail before spending 18 months in a role, you will have failed. Based on the data, there's a 50% chance that you will.

THE FREQUENCY OF EXECUTIVE FAILURE

With failure defined, let's talk about the data.

Overall, the figure I've quoted (a 50% failure rate) is a representative number that's been verified in a number of different studies. You'll be hard-pressed to find anyone who disputes that the executive failure rate sits below 40%; you'll also find some reputable work that suggests the rate might be as high as 70%. I'll offer a brief survey of studies here.

In 2003, Harvard Business School reported that the failure rate for U.S. executives was 40% to 60%.

Michael Watkins, a Harvard professor and the author of 2003's *The First 90 Days*, published research showing that 58% of new executives hired from outside an organization fail within their first 18 months.[2]

In 2009, after internally reviewing the results of

---

2   https://lumenispartners.com/our-approach/a-broken-model/

20,000 executive placements, executive search firm Heidrick & Struggles reported that 40% of executives hired at the senior level were likely to fail within 18 months.

Research by *Corporate Executive Board*[3] (now Gartner) in the 2010s determined that executive failure happened five to seven times for every 10 executive hires.

In 2017, consulting firm Navalent[4] published the results of a 10-year longitudinal study of executive performance. They reported that, on the basis of 2,600 in-depth, qualitative interviews with Fortune 1000 executives, the failure rate sat at between 50% and 70%.

The *Harvard Business Review*, in a 2017 article supporting the Navalent study, cited the same figure[5].

There are more studies, but the main takeaway from all of them is this: The rate of executive

---

3   https://www.cebglobal.com

4   http://navalent.com/

5   https://hbr.org/2017/11/executives-fail-to-execute-strategy-because
     -theyre-too-internally-focused

failure is remarkably consistent. In fact, if anything, it seems to have slightly increased over the past 15 years.

You won't like to hear this, but I think that it will only get worse over the next 15.

The Generational Leadership Gap

Succession planning, when done effectively, takes into consideration the pool of talent in an organization and their respective levels of readiness for taking on a broader (or higher) role. It's a thoughtful process that evaluates the organization's current and future needs and the leaders' skills and growth potential. We find that, as the most senior leaders in organizations voluntarily exit their roles, the next-in-line leaders are, generally speaking, considerably younger. Younger does not mean less prepared, but it may mean less experienced. It also builds the case for intentional and intense professional development. More on that later.

QUICK PRIMER ON THE GENERATIONS:[6]		
GENERATION	BIRTH YEARS	PERCENTAGE OF THE U.S. WORKFORCE
Gen Z, iGen, or Centennials	Born 1996 – TBD	5%
Millennials or Gen Y	Born 1977 – 1995	35%
Generation X	Born 1965 – 1976	33%
Baby Boomers	Born 1946 – 1964	25%
Traditionalists or Silent Generation	Born 1945 and before	2%

What exactly do the numbers look like?

There are about 73 million Baby Boomers in the U.S. Every day, 10,000 of them leave the work-force.[7] This number reflects turnover at all levels

---

6   https://www.pewresearch.org/fact-tank/2018/04/11
     /millennials-largest-generation-us-labor-force/

7   https://www.washingtonpost.com/news/fact-checker/wp/2014/07/24
     /do-10000-baby-boomers-retire-every-day/

of organizations, including the highest levels of
leadership. Boomers are the generation most
likely to hold executive positions. A 2016 study of
the top 1,000 U.S. companies found that the average age of a C-Suite member was 54[8]. CEOs were
likely to be even older, with an average age of 58.
As of 2018, of all CEOs in S&P 500 companies,
80% were Boomers.[9]

Our most senior workers, by tenure and experience, are preparing to retire. By 2028, all Boomers will be at least 63 years of age.

The Gen X population is about half the size of
the Baby Boomer generation. There are twice as
many positions being vacated as there are emerg-
ing leaders to fill them. This means organizations
are having to reach down to younger and younger
leaders to shore up their leadership pipelines.

How do we prepare our Gen X and Millennials
to step into these roles? This group has lived in

---

8   https://www.kornferry.com/about-us/press/age-and-tenure-in-the-c
     -suite-korn-ferry-institute-study-reveals-trends-by-title-and-industry

9   https://insight.factset.com/what-would-a-transfer-of-power-from-baby
     -boomers-to-generation-x-look-like

the shadow of Boomers for years. Baby Boomers, because they're so numerous and because they're staying in the workforce longer than previous generations, have thrown the development of thousands of high-potential, would-be executives out of whack. Career arcs were slow and stymied, and in about a 10-year span, they sped up exponentially.

For Gen Xers, there's now some whiplash: They were road-blocked at first and are now getting pulled up into a leadership vacuum. A 2018 study by consulting firm DDI found that Gen X leaders have advanced up the corporate ladder more slowly than Baby Boomers did.[10] Now, though, with the mass exodus of older leaders, they're being elevated more quickly.

This may be why HBR cites that 61% of executives feel unprepared for new roles. Not *under*prepared—*un*prepared.[11]

---

10   https://www.ddiworld.com/research/the-hidden-potential-of-gen-x-leaders

11   https://hbr.org/2017/11/executives-fail-to-execute-strategy-because
-theyre-too-internally-focused

The Millennial generation is closer in size to the Baby Boomers, so they are guarded from the breakneck speed of ascension that Gen X is facing. But as Gen X is stretched thin, the heavy lifting eventually falls to Millennials. They, too, are rising to leadership positions more quickly than previous generations.

If you're a Gen Xer, there's a good chance that at some point in your career, you found yourself stuck waiting behind a long-sitting Baby Boomer without a chance to put your leadership potential into practice. There's also a good chance that when your path did clear, it did so abnormally quickly, and you were called to step into a leadership role with far less experience than Baby Boomers had at the same age. Naturally, this makes it more likely that you'll fail.

The floodgates have opened. Without the necessary support, the executive failure rate will only increase over the next 15 years.

For Millennials, the situation is similar: They're being promoted far more quickly than usual out of a necessity to fill open seats, and their steep career climbs are robbing them of experience and depressing their likelihood of success. If you're a Millennial, you've been granted fewer cycles of feedback and learning before being asked to lead. That's exciting, but it also makes you more likely to fail.

Despite the challenges, there's still plenty of reason for optimism, because, as I'll lay out over the following pages, a quick transition does not necessarily mean failure. As I have learned working with leaders at all levels, the great majority of executive failures are avoidable. Regardless of what generation you belong to, you can succeed in an executive role.

THE COST OF EXECUTIVE FAILURE

Finally, to understand the problem of executive failure, you have to understand what it costs.

I'm sure you know that failure costs organizations *something*. But you might be surprised to find how much.

Chief Executive, in an article titled "The Costs of CEO Failure," estimates that the customary severance of a CEO is typically three times their annual salary[12]. That's a lot, and it's only a starting point. Company valuation can suffer, too. Booz Allen Hamilton found that replacing a CEO when a company has been doing well produces a negative effect 10.2% worse than average on stock price.

While CEO failure incurs the highest costs, organizations pay a hefty price for losing any senior leader. Research suggests that, overall, companies pay 2.5 times a leader's salary in turnover costs[13]. That includes things like recruiting fees, opportunity costs, productivity losses, and stalled business results. And while that money talks, it still doesn't speak to the weight of the emotional and relational costs that the people within organizations face when executives fail. Executive failure drags down morale and stagnates business results.

---

12 https://chiefexecutive.net/the-costs-of-ceo-failure/

13 http://theleadershipforge.com/2015/09/the-cost-of-failed-leadership
    -and-how-to-avoid-it/

This may be why HBR
cites that 61% of executives feel
unprepared for new roles.
Not underprepared—unprepared.

The customary severance
of a CEO is typically three times
their annual salary.

The Personal Cost of Executive Failure

If you're worried about failing in your new role, though, I'm willing to bet that you're most worried not about the organizational cost of failure, but about the personal cost.

You're worried that failure will cost you.

Recognizing that isn't selfish; it's human. Honestly, the impact of executive failure on an organization pales when it's weighed against the impact of failure on humans.

Executive failure hurts people.

If you're considering taking a new role as an executive, you're considering taking a big risk. You might need to move across the country. Your spouse might need to get a new job. You might need to send your kids to a new school. If you do all of this and you drag your family with you and then you fail, it can be life-shattering. The people you care most about can get hurt.

UNDERSTANDING FAILURE

This is the reality, and it's critical that you understand what you're facing when you enter a new role, especially if it is in an organization or business unit that's new to you. You need the context. If you don't have it—if you don't understand the stakes—you're less likely to take the steps you need to in order to be prepared to succeed.

And that's the good news: You *can* succeed.

Executive failure, given what it is and what it costs, occurs at a disconcerting frequency. But it doesn't have to happen to you. You can drastically reduce the chance that you fail in your new role. You can prepare so that you thrive in it.

I'm going to tell you how.

How I Know
This Stuff

How I Know This Stuff

If you want to dive right into the tactics of reducing new executive failure, skip this chapter and go to Chapter 4. But if you want to know who I am and where I get my information from before you take my advice, I get it.

I'll start with this: I have more than 20 years of hard-won experience in executive consulting.

I'm often asked how I got into consulting in the first place. My first response is always, "I have absolutely no idea." But I do know where the seed was planted. I was taking a class on organizational communication in college with a man who would become the most important mentor of my life: Dave.

Dave was a wonderful lecturer, and the content he was presenting was intriguing. His class dealt with organizational cultures: how values, policies, leadership styles, and physical environments all created different working environments, and where the rationales for different types of culture came from.

I won't go into the nitty gritty of it all, but at 22, I found every word fascinating. Before Dave's class, I was convinced that all employers were awful. Because when I was growing up, my dad had worked for GE.

(Before I go on, you're at a choice point. If you deeply admire Jack Welch, you may not love everything you read in this book. I'm not saying there is nothing to be learned from him. You can learn leadership from anyone... but sometimes it's what *not* to do.)

I grew up in the late '70s. My dad was a machine operator who worked the third shift in a factory that sat in the bad part of town where we lived. He rode his bike to work most days, since we couldn't afford gas for the car we owned. It wasn't a big problem, because the car never ran anyway.

I remember my dad nailing my windows shut when he left for work at night. We didn't have air conditioning, and Indiana summers are oppressively hot and humid, but it was the only way he felt he could keep us safe.

I remember screaming matches about money in our house. My dad always wanted to work, but layoffs became a recurring theme for us through the '80s. Dad always got called back, but we were sometimes food insecure and the money stress was palpable to everyone.

During that time, GE had a culture that was best summed up by the internal slogan, "We eat our young." I'll let you imagine how that saying translated to the guy with no education working the worst job in the worst factory on the worst shift. He was completely demoralized and it was painfully obvious, even to a little kid. It was hard to watch. I wondered, "Why does work have to be this way?"

Because, even at age 6, I *knew* it didn't. Forty years later, I have the proof.

So when I took Dave's class—having only worked retail and waitress jobs myself, none of which would be classified as good work experience—a light went on inside of me. And by light, I mean a bolt of lightning.

I knew. I just knew. I didn't know *how*, but I knew that I wanted to help improve the way that companies are run.

When you have that sense of purpose, honestly, life gets simple.

After I graduated, I went on to work for Dave at the university, where I ran a large academic program for about a decade. During those years I started my firm, basically by stumbling into it.

I often asked Dave to let me help him in his consulting practice (I was dying to learn), but he always said, "Nope!" Eventually, though, he kicked me one consulting job that he didn't want. It was enough. I figured it out, and eventually I left higher education for full-time consulting. That was in 2008, a year in which the economy tanked and I went through an expensive divorce. A good time to give up all security, no? (I do not recommend this.) But after one really lean year, my business bounced back, and today we've done so much more than I dared to imagine.

For the last 20 years, I've run a boutique consulting firm working internationally in everything from Fortune 500s to start-ups. We've helped executives in basically every industry. It's been an incredible run of learning, solving complex problems, and building relationships, which is the best feeling in the world for me.

In the beginning, my work centered around assessing executives. These were typically Directors to CXOs who had failed to assimilate to new cultures or new jobs or new teams. I would come in, analyze the situation, and set forth a development plan to save the executive and help them be successful, when possible. But the thing that always wrenched my gut was that most of the troubles people were in should have been addressed much earlier.

Every weakness in every executive could be tied to some event or shortcoming that showed up in their first six months—and they were still trying to overcome them.

We were typically called in at 12 to 36 months after the hire. That's enough time for the executive to get off on the wrong foot, but not so late in the game that the company couldn't salvage the deal. I still love that work, and we're still strong on that front, but the reality is that it takes a lot of time to unwind the damage executives cause with early missteps. It often takes 12 to 18 months (and sometimes much longer) to fix and redirect everything.

Here's why that matters to me: People hate to fail. I've been there, with the folks who are failing. I've seen their tears. I've witnessed the torment. I've heard the desperation. Most of the time, I can help these people right the ship. But it takes time, and how much time they have to course correct isn't up to me to determine. And it's certainly not up to them.

So when a client asked me if they could solve their (very high) failure rate among officers, I said confidently, "Yes, let's try!"

We've successfully assimilated more than 85 executives. We've interviewed more than 850 people in all levels of organizations to identify what they expect from new leaders.

And that's how I got into executive assimilation.

Six years later, we've successfully assimilated more than 85 executives. We've interviewed more than 850 people in all levels of organizations to identify what they expect from new leaders. We have a tremendous database built around what people want in a new leader. And we have a formula that works for onboarding into executive roles in a strategic, effective way that virtually eliminates the risk of failure.

But in the grand scheme of corporate culture, we've only made a dent: 50% of new executives still fail. Our positive experience with 85 executives isn't enough; more leaders need to understand this precarious moment in their careers.

You can trust my advice because it's hard-won and based on years of real-world study, analysis, and success. And you can trust me when I say that we can do better.

The Three Keys to Success

4

The Three Keys to Success

There's a team-building activity called "The Marshmallow Challenge" that consistently makes executives look like fools. I do not subject clients to this.

You may have seen videos of it online (it's the subject of a popular TED Talk), but if you haven't, here's the gist: Competing small groups (usually of three to five people each) are given a collection of materials: 20 pieces of spaghetti, 20 inches of masking tape, and a marshmallow. They're given an objective: To build a structure that is both as tall as possible *and* capable of supporting the weight of the marshmallow at its very top. And they're given a timeframe: They have to accomplish this task within five minutes.

Here's what happens:

The teams of intelligent businesspeople spend the first minutes jockeying for power. They debate among themselves how to build the structure. When they've finally sorted things out enough to agree on a plan, they start building a tower.

At first, things seem to go well.

A tower built of spaghetti and tape rises from each team's table. The groups build determinedly, only stopping to glance anxiously at other tables as they estimate and compare the height of various towers against their own. The structures grow. The timer ticks down. The tension is palpable.

Then, usually with under a minute left, the teams proceed to place the marshmallow at the pinnacle of their constructions.

At this point, chaos breaks out.

The weight of the marshmallow causes the structures to bend, then break, then collapse. Grins turn to groans. As the buzzer sounds, 80% of the teams are fussing over a tower that's in shambles. There may be one or two lucky teams

whose structures hold; everyone else is left
with a marshmallow sitting on top of a pile of
snapped spaghetti.

It's pretty funny. It's also instructive.

There are a lot of lessons baked into this activity, but here's what is helpful in our context:
These executives fail because they misunder-
stand the factors involved in successfully com-
pleting the objective.

They don't realize how quickly five minutes will
pass, so they don't use their time wisely. They
don't understand the social dynamics of their
group, so they waste energy debating who's
in charge. And they don't accurately gauge the
weight of the marshmallow, so their towers break.

The bottom line is that when you don't understand the factors that are critical to your success,
you won't succeed.

But when teams try this challenge a second time,
they understand these things—and they're nearly
always able to build a tower that far surpasses

their previous effort. Because they understand the factors they're bound by, they can achieve their objective.

This is a simple exercise, but it represents the approach that many executives take as they enter into new roles. New executives too often *assume* that they know what's expected of them—that they know what will impact their success. But, as "The Marshmallow Challenge" shows, naive assumptions tend to get crushed under the weight of reality. If you want to succeed, you need to *truly* know the factors that will impact your success.

I have some good news.

I've spent years assimilating nearly 100 new-to-role executives. Over the course of that experience, I've learned that there are three key factors to navigate in a new executive position: The charter, the culture, and the team. These are the considerations new executives are bound by.

THE CHARTER

Your charter is what your organization expects you to accomplish in your new role. While it may not explicitly lay out a timeframe within which you need to hit your goals, it almost certainly has expectations built in.

THE CULTURE

An HBR *deep-dive into company culture defines it as "the tacit social order of an organization," and notes that "cultural norms define what is encouraged, discouraged, accepted, or rejected within a group." At a basic level, your business's culture is its way of doing things.*

THE TEAM

This definition is straightforward: Your team is the group of people under your leadership.

If you understand each of these factors—and, again, I mean truly understand them, not simply *assume* you understand them—then, just like the Marshmallow Challenge teams undertaking the activity for the second time, you'll be able to develop and act on an effective strategy that will allow you to accomplish your objectives.

I'll spend the following three chapters unpacking the intricacies of each factor. For each one, I'll provide you with proven frameworks to assess and act on what matters. Follow the roadmap outlined in the pages ahead, and you'll almost certainly be able to avoid an outcome that's a pile of wreckage.

Let's start with the charter.

The Charter

The Charter

Having an understanding of your charter is like having self-awareness: Everyone thinks they've got it, but only the people who've done the work actually do.

Too often, new executives haven't done the work. They enter new roles without truly understanding their charters. This makes them more likely to fail.

Of course, as a new leader, the responsibility to clarify your charter shouldn't rest entirely on your shoulders. Largely, it should rest with the organization you're entering. In a perfect world, companies would align their charters internally before hiring, then communicate them clearly so new hires would know exactly what to expect.

We don't live in a perfect world, unfortunately. That almost never happens.

Instead, you're likely to be oversold on the upsides of a role and undersold on its challenges during the hiring process. And while your direct manager may tell you what they expect from you, you probably won't be able to synthesize that with what's expected from your board and your business partners and peers.

In fact, when you enter a new role, it's unlikely that all of the organization's internal stakeholders have taken the time to codify and align expectations for what you should accomplish in it. Most new leaders sit down in seats where the definition of success is subject to ongoing debate.

Usually, the fact that a charter hasn't been settled isn't obvious upfront. I worked, for example, with a Chief Data Officer at a large bank, who was handed what seemed to be a clear charter from his CEO. He was tasked with accomplishing $1.5 billion in savings in his department through the enactment of several major initiatives over a certain amount of time. It was all very clearly defined, which was encouraging. As the icing on the cake, he was promised that he'd have access to any resources he would need to make it happen.

It seemed ideal. But it wasn't the full picture.

Instead, as he entered into the role, he found that the charter the CEO handed him didn't match the reality of organizational expectations. His business partners were not going to accept the amount of change he was tasked with accomplishing within the timeframe he was tasked to accomplish it. The result was that none of his initiatives could go through, and any assurances that this was the CEO's top priority were only met with more contempt. Contempt, resistance, and noise all create drag—it's like walking through chest-deep water. You can do it, but not forever, and it's exhausting and slow.

It didn't matter how many resources the new CDO had at his disposal; there was a cultural ceiling that was smothering his charter. The executive ended up unable to meet his CEO's ambitious goals. It wasn't long until he left the company to find a better position with more realistic expectations of what's truly possible.

The reality is that your charter is not just what your manager tells you it is; it's what the organization, *cumulatively*, expects you to accomplish, and it's the pace at which they expect you to accomplish it.

And because a charter is cumulative in nature, there's only one way to fully understand it.

HOW TO CLARIFY WHAT YOUR CHARTER REALLY IS

To understand your charter—and give yourself the best chance of succeeding in your new role— you'll need to talk to more than just your CEO or your boss.

You'll need to talk to every key stakeholder.

This includes:
- Your boss(es)
- Your peers
- Your direct reports
- Any relevant business partners
- Cross-functional partners
- And others

As you speak with these people, you should be seeking to uncover two primary points of information:

 ## HOW MUCH CHANGE IS NEEDED

This is an extrapolation of the question, "What does success in this role look like?" It compares the ideal outcome for your prospective role against the current state you'll be inheriting.

You should understand what metrics will be evaluated to determine your success, what numbers you'll need to hit to determine that you've succeeded, and how those numbers compare to the team's current performance. Success may not always be strictly quantifiable, of course. But this approach is a good place to start.

To identify how much change will be needed and how much will be possible, you should ask questions like these:

- What are the changes you'd like to see in my function?
- How much change has the organization already been through?

- How has morale been affected by the
  changes the org has seen in recent years?
- How high is the org's appetite for additional change?
- In an ideal world, what does this function
  look like in three years?

Note that some of these questions are redun-
dant, but that can be necessary. Different
questions spark different insights for different
people. Reframe the same idea in different
ways to give your people multiple avenues to
hear and respond.

② HOW LONG IS THE TIME HORIZON?

The second data point you'll need to account
for is how long you have to accomplish your
objectives.

Often, this is murky. It's not uncommon for organizations to have more clarity on the metrics
that determine success than on the timeframe
for accomplishing the numbers. There are
almost certainly time-based assumptions baked

into a role—most people will probably agree that things need to happen quickly if you're tasked with a turnaround or, if you're stepping into a stable position, that there's no rush. But there's likely to be internal debate over *exactly* how long you really have.

Does "no rush" mean three years? Or does it mean one?

The question you need to ask here is pretty simple—"How long do I have to achieve results?"—but the key is to ask it to *all* stakeholders in order to get a true understanding of the answer.

It's important to get crystal clear on this. You can't plan to take off if all you know is that you need to reach 30,000 feet. You also need to know the length of the runway.

THE FIVE TYPES OF CHARTERS

The answers you uncover from stakeholders will allow you to plot your new role on the following quadrant, using the two data points we've noted as the axes. In the chart below, the X axis represents the amount of time you have and the Y axis represents how much change you'll need to enact to succeed.

As you can see, using these two variables as a framework, there are five general types of charters—and different things will be required from you in each type.

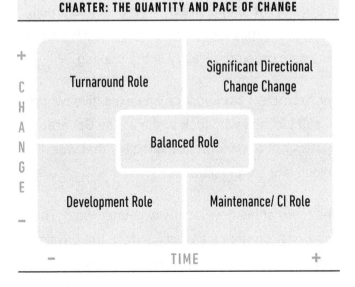

CHARTER: THE QUANTITY AND PACE OF CHANGE

Turnaround Role

Significant Directional
Change Change

Balanced Role

Development Role

Maintenance/ CI Role

C H A N G E

TIME

Let's unpack what you'll need to know should you choose to accept one of these missions.

The Turnaround Charter

Turnaround charters are, arguably, the most difficult charters to fulfill. You're required to execute a lot of change in a short amount of time—usually within nine months to two years, depending on the size of the ship you're steering—and you're often starting from behind, from a place of crisis. Few people are at their best in a crisis, so tensions may very well run high and turnover may be a problem already in the making.

For example, I worked with one executive (whom I'll call Lincoln) who took a role as the General Manager at a manufacturing facility that was, objectively, doing terribly.

The team at his new facility was underpaid. The work environment was dirty. In fact, the Environmental Protection Agency was on the facility's case for compliance issues. Results were bad. Understandably, morale was on the floor.

Lincoln's firm had bought the company from family ownership, and in this case, "family-owned" hadn't lived up to its typical positive connotations. The previous owner had ruled with an iron fist. He'd made every decision, from high-level strategy choices, to capital expenditures, to deciding whether the office would have #2 or #3 pencils.

The situation was tough. Lincoln was given about two years to make it better and generate a $10 million increase in profits.

The good news was that Lincoln's firm—the company that had bought out the declining facility—was great. It was employee-centric, with a clean working environment, environmentally conscious work practices, a positive culture, and high morale. People loved working there. And, importantly for Lincoln, while his bosses had challenging goals for him to meet in his new role, they also offered him support.

What Lincoln found was that his new team was initially skeptical about *all* leadership—and that included the acquiring company and Lincoln himself. They'd been trained to expect the worst.

So instead of enforcing a great degree of change off the bat, we worked with Lincoln to focus on winning the hearts and minds of the people in the plant. He started by showing his team the benefits of the acquisition in tangible ways. Money was infused into the plant and resources that were lacking, like machinery and operational improvements, were added. Over time, his new team was able to see that Lincoln was sincerely interested in making things better. None of the changes he made were punitive, so it was hard for them to stay skeptical.

As people began to trust Lincoln, he was able to increase his expectations for production, and his people were open to meeting the challenges.

Today, the turnaround is virtually complete. The plant is achieving the results Lincoln and his bosses had hoped for, and its culture is worlds better than it was in the early days. This wasn't done by ramming an agenda through a discouraged team; it was done by carefully building people up so that they could achieve stronger results over time.

Sometimes, the slow way *is* the fast way.

With that said, it is true that in a turnaround situation an authoritarian style can be effective—and sometimes it's simply required. It comes down to the level of talent you inherit. If your new talent is bad, you'll need to be more authoritarian. If, though, your team is simply discouraged and there *is* reasonable talent to draw on, you'll do well to be more authoritative than authoritarian. Lead with authority, but bring in the voices of others and gain their perspectives to get buy-in.

Turnarounds are daunting, but they aren't impossible, especially when they're done strategically. If your charter requires a turnaround, you will need to move quickly to evaluate the other two factors in your role (culture and team) and identify the most impactful changes you can make.

The appeal of this role is that you'll get a chance to play the hero, but the stakes are high—and the failure rates are, too.

Sometimes, the slow way *is* the fast way.

The Development Charter

When you receive a development charter, you're not expected to make a high degree of change, and you're not expected to be in the role for the long term.

There are two reasons you may find yourself assigned this type of charter. The first is that you're being asked to serve as a stop-gap; maybe a long-time leader left and the organization wants to pause to evaluate things before committing to a new direction. Or maybe there's a gap that needs to be filled to avert a crisis, and the organization is simply looking to buy some time.

The second reason you might be chosen for a development charter is because the organization wants to develop your leadership capacity. This may be a role where you'll be asked to expand your skill set, prove your leadership ability, or gain visibility into different aspects of the business before being moved to your next post.

In either case, if your charter is a development one, you must realize that major change isn't needed, and pushing for a great deal of change may only create unnecessary noise. Noise costs time, risks your reputation, and arouses unnecessary resistance. If the charter does not require significant change, don't manufacture it.

This might sound like an easy ask. But one of my few assimilation failures happened in a development role.

Julia was in her late 20s, fiery and brilliant. She was tagged as a high-potential leader, and when a beloved CFO stepped down, she was picked for the seat so that she could mature. Her organization wanted her to develop an executive presence and improve her business savvy so that she could lead effectively in the future.

They didn't want much to change in the present. They could take the risk on Julia because the function was strong and could offset her inexperience.

Julia's boss believed things were going wonderfully, and she didn't like to be disagreed with. Unfortunately (for this role), Julia saw herself as a "disrupter." She was the kind of person who, on her first day back from maternity leave, marched into HR to pick a fight over how ridiculous the organization's parental leave policies were. She had a good heart; she wanted to affect positive change. She didn't want to sit on her hands.

But her charter called for her to.

We counseled her to be less disruptive. But it was impossible for her to take that approach. So she led in a way that would have suited a turnaround. She made big changes, created resistance, broke down relationships, and got fired.

If she'd accepted what her charter required of her, she probably wouldn't have taken the role. Or she would have utilized the opportunity for what it was: a chance to grow, mature, gain experience, and prepare for something bigger.

If *you* can handle sitting on your hands, though, this can be a valuable seat to take, as it's a great place to develop your skills and build your brand.

In most development roles, your team will be strong, so rely on your talent. Build up the people under you—make development and promotion of your team a focus. Seek opportunities to gain exposure to higher-level leaders, and take on projects that can build your reputation. This is where a selfless leader can shine.

Your job is to hold down the fort and prove your competency until the cavalry arrives, not to organize a charge.

The Maintenance Charter

Maintenance roles become available when previous executives leave on good terms. In these contexts, it *is* expected that you'll be in the position for the long term, but it's not expected that you'll bring too much upheaval to your team. You'll have time to become familiar with your people and objectives, and you won't need to change them too much.

As with a development role, a maintenance role sounds easy on its surface. But for executives who like to have a high degree of control or who want to see a notable impact from their leadership, maintenance charters can be frustrating. You'll need to be prepared to learn the status quo of your team and culture and then lead from there. You'll need to avoid rocking the boat too early or often.

To do this effectively, be congenial. Your aim is to help work function smoothly; often, this involves collaborating with cross-functional partners. Focus on continuous improvement and small, incremental, positive changes.

Ideal maintenance-role leaders personify quiet, subtle, servant leadership. They're Steady Eddies. They're stabilizers. They're not working so much on themselves; they're just keeping stuff working.

If you're a change agent, you will suck at this. Be careful.

The Strategic Change Charter

Strategic change roles carry expectations for seismic change but, unlike in a turnaround position, you'll be granted the opportunity to accomplish that change over an extended period of time—usually two to three years or more.

This kind of charter is a good fit if you're a visionary.

While it's crucial in any role, stakeholder buy-in is the ultimate object for a directional change charter. You will need to take time to understand the status quo of your team and culture, then guide your people to move past it. A collaborative approach—one where stakeholders are empowered to shape the vision—can be effective.

Highly charismatic leaders do well in this setting. To succeed, you'll need to inspire and give people a reason to believe in something that's different and better. Unlike in a turnaround position, however, you'll need to be conscientious about the endurance you're requiring from your team. This role is a diligent push over a period of time. In the end, you'll achieve a volume of change similar to what would have been accomplished in a turnaround, but it will happen over a three- to five-year journey.

So don't come in heavy-handed—you'll squash morale. Build an environment people want to be a part of for the long haul and include their voices in your vision of the future.

Be confident and charismatic. Don't be a jerk.

The Balanced Charter

When you receive a balanced charter, you'll be expected to implement some degree of change in a middling amount of time.

Balanced roles are the most gray. They're also the most common.

Importantly, you should stay away from polarizing decisions and behaviors. As in most roles, collaboration, cooperation, and continuous improvement work here. Take the time to invest in your people and your team. Cultivate a reputation as a strong people-leader.

If you accept a role with a balanced charter, it will be even more essential for you to understand

your team and your culture—the other two factors in your success. You'll likely weigh those
components more heavily as you make decisions.

THE POINT OF UNDERSTANDING YOUR CHARTER

And that's what all of this comes down to: decision making.

If you know what your organization expects
of you, you can make decisions that align with
those expectations. If you don't know—or you
only *kind of* know—you'll make the wrong decisions or you'll make the wrong trade-offs. You
can't make too many of those before people lose
faith in you. That's when failure begins. You can
spend your whole life building credibility—but
you can lose it in a nanosecond. This is where
most executives stumble. Failing to truly understand the perspectives of all of the stakeholders
your actions will affect makes it impossible to
predict (let alone control for) the impact of your
day-to-day decision making.

Two final notes before we move on to the next factor: First, as you evaluate whether or not to accept a new role, it's important to recognize your own strengths and skills as a leader and evaluate how they might fit (or not fit) the charter before you.

If you are a slow and steady, relationally oriented person, for example, you probably won't be well-served by accepting a high-stakes turnaround role. Similarly, if you thrive in the midst of fast-paced, constantly innovating environments, you may want to be careful about accepting a role that requires long-term, directional change.

Second, though, you should be prepared to adapt your leadership style toward what your charter *requires.* One of the most common mistakes that new leaders make is to fail to do this. We all have a preferred leadership style, but it needs to shift to align with what's needed, *not what we prefer.*

Here's the truth: You will never be a perfect fit for a new role. Perfect fits don't exist.

So don't be inflexible in your approach. You shouldn't take a position that requires you to shove a square peg into a round hole, but you should expect that you'll be asked to whittle down a few of your corners.

When you understand what your charter requires—how much change is expected and how long you have to accomplish it—you'll be better prepared to craft an approach that works.

You will never be a perfect fit
for a new role. Perfect fits don't exist.

The Culture

The Culture

The second crucial factor to understand as you enter your new role is your new organization's culture. Culture is what people and organizations care about. Misalignment to culture is one of the biggest reasons new leaders fail.

Unfortunately, cultures are notoriously difficult to decipher.

For one thing, they're subjective. Different people within a culture may have different understandings of what their culture is—they may care about different things or find different things important. And it's difficult to measure cultural tendencies, whereas it's much easier to measure things like profit margins or salary offers.

Additionally, the reality of culture is often obscured by people's intentions. We've all been in places that have preached core values in public and have practiced opposing behaviors in private.

As a new-to-role executive, you're likely to be spoon-fed the public image of the culture during your hiring and onboarding processes. You'll be shown the house when it's cleaned up for company, but you won't find out about the crazy uncle or the junk drawer until you join the family.

Finally, culture varies significantly from company to company—and even from team to team—which can lead to misguided assumptions. As humans, we tend to automatically operate as if the culture we're familiar with is the normal one. It's not. Just like your childhood friends' parents had different rules for what was rewarded and what wasn't tolerated within the family, your new employer does, too. And those rules are hard to understand until you spend every single day living by them.

Those rules can be downright weird, too.

I was once asked, for example, to coach the executives of a large oncology practice that was somewhat unhealthy. The leaders were talented doctors and pugnacious people; they'd built the business on the basis of their medical skills and had driven it to a place where leadership development had become impossible to ignore.

They were aggressive.

And that was their core problem: In their culture, decisions were determined based on who argued the loudest. Meetings tended to be displays of passion with blaring disagreement over budget, or personnel, or strategy, or anything of consequence, really. It was an angry environment, so much so that it wasn't uncommon for an argument to end in someone throwing a chair. That person was usually the winner of the debate.

If you're wondering—no, I didn't take that engagement. Some things are simply above my pay grade.

On the other end of the spectrum, I've been in places where conflict or rigorous debate was seemingly nonexistent; meetings were rubber-stamp formalities where everyone was expected to agree. Any disagreement happened in private, which often meant that misalignment wasn't truly dealt with. Golf-clapping was considered aggressive.

People are strange in all possible ways.

The point here is that culture varies, and you need to understand your organization's rules before you play its game. A leader entering that oncology practice with a collaborative, people-oriented approach would've been eaten alive. A leader with the desire to encourage discussions of diverse ideas would struggle to acclimate to a conflict-averse culture. And these things aren't always obvious. Culture is tricky to comprehend until you live it.

But don't panic. As with your charter, there's a specific set of questions to ask that will quickly reveal culture to you.

Here's what you should be looking to understand as you enter your new role:

① WHAT DO THE MOST SUCCESSFUL LEADERS HERE CARE ABOUT MOST?

Identifying the answer to this question is perhaps the single fastest way to figure out what an organization's culture is like. If you know what gets rewarded by the people at the top, you'll know what drives the culture.

For example, if you ask this question and the response you get is, "Well, our executives are usually pretty willing to take risks even when they go against industry norms," you can start to frame your new culture as innovative and progressive. On the other hand, if you hear something like, "Results get rewarded because what's most important here is winning," you'll know to expect more of a cutthroat culture.

As with your charter, getting a well-rounded perspective on this is essential. The more people you pose this question to, the more likely you'll be to get an accurate picture of what your new cultural norms really are.

(2) WHEN PEOPLE HERE FAIL, WHAT'S TYPICALLY THE CAUSE?

This one can be a little bit more uncomfortable to ask, but it can lead to crucial insights.

People usually fail for one of two reasons: Either they fail to achieve business results, or they fail to achieve results in a culturally acceptable way.

If, in your new role, you learn that most people fail for the first reason, it's likely that your organization values the bottom line above all else, and you can make your leadership decisions accordingly. In this case, the culture may not value building relationships or working collaboratively—those attributes may be considered weaknesses. If, though, you learn that creating too much noise or making cultural missteps are primary reasons for failure (i.e., "he or she just didn't fit in"), you should be careful to study and adhere to your organization's ways of doing things for a time. Employees probably value their culture, and therefore you should move a tad more slowly and observe it carefully.

By identifying where the boundary lines are, you can make sure that you stay within them.

③ WHAT'S AN EARLY MISTAKE PEOPLE IN SIMILAR ROLES MAKE, AND HOW CAN I AVOID IT?

In this final question, you'll get more specific and gather some great historical context.

Did the person before you burn out quickly? Did another leader rock the boat too much when stepping into a tightly knit team? Did a previous boss fail to communicate their preferences or fail to provide context for key decisions?

How a company defines *what* a mistake is will reveal a lot about its culture. Learning about the specific situations that led to previous failures will help you decide how to assimilate—and how not to.

CULTURAL SPECTRUMS

As you gather information by asking the questions above, it's helpful to have frameworks for understanding the culture you're entering. While culture is hard to define, there are spectrums that can provide points of reference.

Here are a few that I've found to be most impact-ful. This list isn't exhaustive, of course, but it is a good starting point:

CULTURE: THE WAY LEADERS ARE EXPECTED TO LEAD		
Cooperative	⬅➡	Competitive
Humble	⬅➡	Self-Promoting
Traditional	⬅➡	Innovative
Passive	⬅➡	Aggressive
People-emphasis	⬅➡	Results-emphasis
Transparent	⬅➡	Secretive

Competitive vs. Collaborative

In a competitive culture, individualistic high achievers get rewarded (sometimes at the cost of others). In a collaborative culture, people who work well in teams tend to thrive and good teams are rewarded together.

Humble vs. Self-Promoting

In a humble culture, leaders are quick to distribute credit to others and are willing to admit mistakes. Self-deprecation is acceptable. In a self-promoting culture, people focus on communicating their achievements and are quick to take credit when they can, sometimes for the work of others. Self-deprecation is a sign of weakness.

Traditional vs. Innovative

In a traditional culture, the people who play within the lines are admired. There's a resistance to change, even if it might achieve better results. In an innovative culture, ideas are rewarded. Employees are encouraged to try new things, even if the results aren't guaranteed. Fast failure, iterative working, and innovation are the order of the day in companies like this.

Passive vs. Aggressive

In a passive culture, disagreement is viewed as conflict, conversations are quiet, and judgments on ideas aren't usually made in public. In an aggressive culture, meetings are loud, different viewpoints are seen as pathways to better results, and ideas get bluntly critiqued. (I've also had client cultures I would describe as passive-aggressive. It's crazy-making.)

People Emphasis vs. Results Emphasis

In organizations with a people emphasis, *how* things are done matters as much as, or even more than, what the outcomes are. These supportive cultures value personal growth and skill development. In a results-first organization, on the other hand, you'd be committing a cultural faux pas if you took an accommodating approach to a poor performer.

Transparent vs. Secretive

In a transparent culture, honesty is rewarded and questions are encouraged. Most people know most things that are going on and meetings are fairly open. Informational power is shared with many. In a secretive culture, insights are closely guarded. There are clear (if unspoken) rules about who gets access to what information, and backroom conversations are the norm. Informational power is held by a few.

Hierarchical vs. Non-Hierarchical

In a hierarchical culture, there's a clear pecking order, and it's crucial to identify the people above and below you in the chain of command and get their buy-in if you want to move an agenda. In a non-hierarchical culture, you'll have more free rein to do what you want, with less formal decision making and fewer gatekeepers to those layers above or below you. The downside is less clarity in decision-making rights.

THE POINT OF UNDERSTANDING YOUR CULTURE

Assessing your culture correctly and assimilating to its norms are both crucial to succeeding in your new role—especially when you are still making an impression, building credibility, and strengthening your internal connections.

Like an organ transplant that fails because the new tissue doesn't match its surroundings, if you don't align your leadership style to the culture you're entering, you'll be quickly rejected. You need to fit in, *enough*, to reassure others that you're one of them.

I do realize that this advice to assimilate might place a new executive in a stressful double bind, especially as a member of an under-represented group. I have felt that bind myself. In time, you can let the *true you* come through and push the edges of cultural norms. Do that on your first day and it's too soon; on your last day it's too late. Establish yourself, build trust, demonstrate results. Then you can start to rebel against the culture.

This will take work on your part. You may find yourself in a role that's on the other side of a spectrum from your previous position. Maybe you came from a startup and are tasked with leading a team at a larger enterprise; you'd better quickly identify how traditional your culture is before you innovate your way out of your job. Maybe you came from a culture where honesty was admired and ideas were subject to judgment, but your new team values cooperation and politeness more than meaningful debate.

Identify and adapt. Don't rush in blindly.

I've seen too many executives make this mistake. One, whom I'll call Meghan, was a new HR manager who inherited a long-neglected function of learning and development. She came from a company with a very aggressive culture and, at a personal level, she carried a bit of a chip on her shoulder for reasons unknown.

Unfortunately, the culture she was trying to assimilate into was collegial, cooperative, and somewhat resistant to change. The way to integrate into a culture like this is to talk, ask questions, and learn.

Meghan didn't adapt, and so she came across as a controlling, rude, demanding bully with something to prove.

She should have assessed her function carefully by meeting with key stakeholders, vendors, and colleagues to discover what people loved, what frustrated them, and what they aspired to.

Instead, she refused to meet with anyone but her own boss. She aggressively fired all existing vendors and charted an unprecedented course, moving from boutique, high-touch vendors to large vendors—despite what senior leaders preferred. The unintended impact was that she prematurely stopped ongoing coaching engagements and erected a firewall between vendors and the clients they were retained to serve.

As a result, the first impression her new organization's most senior leaders had of her was that she was the person who'd taken away something they valued. Many leaders asked, "Who is she, anyway?" Meghan was only a Senior Manager; it was hard for C-level execs to understand how she was able to make the changes she did. But she had her own manager's support, so she went for broke, firing everyone and bringing in all-new, unknown programs.

Meghan made three crucial cultural mistakes:

1. She misjudged the readiness within her new organization for change because she didn't perform her due diligence.
2. She took away things that people loved instead of assessing and addressing real pain points, which alienated her from top leaders.
3. She didn't realize that the organization's leaders would give her enough rope to hang herself—but they did.

While she was successful at integrating the changes *she* wanted, she failed to address actual needs. Ultimately, after about three years, she had lost whatever political capital she had brought with her and found it difficult to gain respect, trust, and partnerships within the business. She'd created unnecessary noise, broken trust, and created ill will. And she'd done it all in a culturally unacceptable way.

If you take anything from this book, make it this:

Don't be Meghan.

Instead, demonstrate that you fit into your new team with behaviors that align to their culture. You'll earn their respect as you gain their trust.

When you've built a strong relationship with your team, you'll be in a position to effectively lead them.

The Team

The Team

The third and final factor you'll need to accurately gauge in your new role is the state of your team. For our purposes, the team is the group of people under your leadership. In large part, these folks will enable your success or failure. You need to lead them, and to do that, you need to understand them.

As with the other factors, getting this right can be tricky.

WHAT YOU NEED TO UNDERSTAND ABOUT YOUR TEAM

Teams are made of people, and people are messy. But I have good news: When we talk about understanding your team, we're talking about understanding two primary factors: their morale and their talent.

Yes, both of these factors are nuanced. But once you know what you're looking for, finding the right answers is easier.

The State of Morale

At a basic level, morale is how people feel about working where they're working. High morale means that they feel passionate, dedicated, fulfilled, and rewarded. They believe they're treated fairly, and they're generally aligned with the organization's actions and objectives.

It's not just about happiness, though. Kevin P. Coyne, writing for *HBR* in 2007 on the precipice of the Great Recession, clarifies the idea of morale:

> *Good morale does not require people to be happy. The definition of good morale is that people's emotions contribute to, rather than subtract from, the unit achieving its goals. Many of the best examples of high morale come from situations of great unhappiness and stress—such as heroic actions in war, etc. Thus, while it may be*

*impossible to make people feel happy while
their friends are being let go, that is not
your job. Your job is to build your team's
focus and dedication.*[14]

As you step into a new role, then, there are two
questions you'll need to ask yourself in order to
identify the state of your team's morale. "Is my
team happy?" is not one of them.

Instead, ask:

1. What are the mental and emotional states
    of the individuals on my team?
2. Are those states contributing to or detract-
    ing from my team's ability to hit its goals—
    and to what degree?

In what you've probably identified as a common
theme over the previous two chapters, you'll only
be able to answer these critical questions for
yourself if you talk to enough of the right people.

You need to gauge the temperature of your team.

---

14 https://hbr.org/2007/12/building-morale-when-times-are

Obviously, you can't ask about morale directly. Sitting down and asking, "On a scale from one to 10, how high is your morale?" would typecast you as a weirdo. Instead, you'll need to come at this from the side, then pull themes together.

Here are a few questions that I recommend asking:

 **WHAT HAVE THE LAST THREE YEARS BEEN LIKE?**

If the general sense you get is that the past few years have been amazing, your team probably has high morale. If people have mostly negative stories to tell, you're probably dealing with a low-morale group. Listen for content and tone— teams can describe a major challenge, but if the challenge brought them together or yielded learning or success, they may have a positive attitude about the challenge. If work is "easy" and the team has not been stretched, then you'll detect a pessimistic vibe. Hollow victories ("Our boss didn't care what we did!") don't always inspire high morale, even though work is easy.

(2) WHAT ARE THE BIGGEST CHALLENGES THIS TEAM HAS BEEN THROUGH IN THE PAST FIVE MONTHS?

If the story is, "Things were going really great and then our boss left; now, we're really upset and it sort of blows that you're here," then your new team probably has a fragile morale at the moment. Your actions will have a high impact. Don't worry, teams aren't usually this honest. But it is possible that your predecessor was beloved. That, in and of itself, can crush morale for a time, no matter how good you may be.

(3) WHAT ARE THREE CHANGES YOU WOULD MAKE TO HOW WE WORK?

This question will tell you what's important to your team and what's not working well for them. If they'd only change the little stuff ("We should move the weekly status meeting to Wednesdays"), then the important things are probably okay. If you get something more substantive ("We need to integrate with other departments more effectively, because projects keep blowing up"), you may have bigger issues.

The answers will take work to uncover and unpack. But they'll be crucial in informing how you navigate decisions with your team.

Talent

The second factor that will shape how you handle your team is their level of talent.

Most people find it far more appealing to step into a role on a team that's talented than to try to fix a team that isn't. It's fun to coach a Super Bowl winner. It's harder to coach a bottom-dweller. Most teams tend to fall somewhere in the middle.

Talent is about more than just winning, of course; teams can hit business objectives and not be talented, and talented teams can certainly fail. If talent isn't synonymous with performance, then what exactly do we mean by the word?

The term can be broken down in a few ways, but generally, talent combines natural ability, learned mastery, commitment and/or motivation, and level of fit.

Tomas Chamorro-Premuzic, writing in *HBR*, simplifies it further: "Star organizational players tend to have higher levels of ability, likability, and drive."[15]

It's worth noting that, in an extrapolation of the ongoing debate over the roles of nature and nurture, there are different opinions on the role of organizations in shaping talent. Some people view talent as primarily an individual trait; others view talent as primarily a question of fit within context.

Deloitte, in an article on the aging of the US workforce, recounts the story of an industrial products manufacturer that was faced with the imminent retirement of 70% of its engineering workforce.[16]

---

15 https://hbr.org/2016/10/talent-matters-even-more-than-people-think

16 https://www2.deloitte.com/us/en/insights/focus/technology-and-the
     -future-of-work/redesigning-work-for-our-aging-workforce.html

Instead of simply intensifying its recruiting efforts, the company decided to change its work environment in a way that would not only help new engineers become more productive sooner, but lessen the need for new engineering talent in the first place.

In other words, by changing the definition of a role, you can change the definition of talent in that role.

Here's the long and short of it: Talent is a cumulative representation of a person's ability to accomplish a given role. To evaluate it on your team, you need to know what each role requires and each person's capacity to fill it.

Again, you'll need to have conversations and collect information to get this right. At the most basic level, you'll want to interview your team members about their own capabilities. You'll be looking to find out:

- What their results have been
- Who they've worked for
- What they see as the biggest things to work on moving forward

- What their most pressing challenges are and what they're doing to work through them

These questions should illuminate to some degree how well they have been doing and how you can expect them to perform in the future. If, for example, you think the challenges they've laid out are more excuses than issues, you may have a talent problem. On the other hand, if your new team is displaying ingenuity in solving big issues, you may have high talent regardless of past results.

Of course, most people are generous in gauging their own talent level. So your next step should be to get additional feedback from cross-functional peers or bosses. Here you can be more direct in asking about job performance. As always, it's important to ask enough people and to keep your questions consistent so that you gather similar information from multiple sources.

From there, you can choose to promote, fire, train, or role-change the people on your new team. But no matter what, you'll need to get talent evaluation right to make the correct decisions. Talent calibrations don't happen in a vacuum for a reason: You'll need others to help you learn what your people are capable of. Keep in mind, your predecessor may not have brought out the best in some of them. Develop an understanding of talent through questions about the past, while remaining open-minded about current performance, until you feel confident in your assessment. Take your time, but not forever.

FIVE TYPES OF TEAMS

Once you've evaluated your team's morale and talent, you can determine your strategy. Just as we used a chart to evaluate your charter, we can use a similar chart to evaluate your team. Here, your X axis will be team morale, and your Y axis will be the strength of their talent.

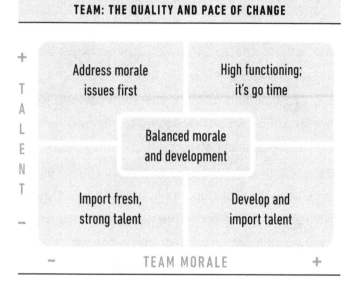

Where your team lies according to these two variables will shape your leadership approach.

High Talent, Low Morale

Teams with high talent and low morale have the capacity for success but have mental or emotional baggage.

Typically, teams that fall into this quadrant have been hurt by a person or situation outside their influence. They may have just emerged from a bad leader (your predecessor, perhaps), or they may have been dealt a tough hand by unrealistic organizational initiatives or some challenging industry event.

The good news is that if you can improve morale, you can improve results. This is what Roy, the executive assimilation client I described in Chapter 1, quickly identified as his first and highest priority.

There are two tactics to take that can boost morale:

First, remove unnecessary work. By doing this, you'll set your talented team up to win at what matters, avoid bogging them down with what doesn't, and clarify what talent means on your team. So often, new leaders launch new initiatives, and those initiatives are never closed out as the next round of leaders (with their own new initiatives) arrive on the scene. Multiply that tendency over the course of four to five recent leaders ... and you have a lot of low-value work that may not even be relevant anymore. Clear it out of the way.

Second, foster productivity by celebrating wins as they happen. Many teams with low morale have been chastised far more than they've been celebrated. Don't be disingenuous and make an unrealistically big deal out of trivial things, but do take the time to notice progress as it's made. What we focus on improves, so focus on wins while acknowledging and learning from losses.

Be encouraged and encouraging.

Low Talent, Low Morale

If you're stepping into a new role with a team that has low morale and low talent—look out.

These assignments are usually very difficult. That's even more true if you're required to execute change quickly.

Really, there's only one thing you can do: Repurpose, rehome, and redevelop your talent as quickly and effectively as you can. You'll need to export some talent and import strong, fresh talent if you want to have any chance at succeeding.

You'll be able to redirect the skills of some B- and C-players, but you'll need to make tough decisions, too.

Be courageous.

High Morale, Low Talent

This is an interesting scenario.

If you feel like your team doesn't have the capacity to succeed but the people are doing well emotionally and mentally, you're in a tricky place. In the culture you're entering, it's likely that business results have taken a backseat to people's feelings. Consequently, you don't want to blow everything up, because you'll risk being rejected. But you also don't want to let the status quo continue until the lack of results becomes too obvious to ignore. Their performance is largely what you'll be evaluated on, so take that seriously.

There's a middle ground here. You'll want to import new talent to demonstrate what you're looking for. You'll also want to increase expectations for legacy

employees. Ideally, turning up expectations gradually is easier for people to accept. (Remember the
analogy of the frog and boiling water.) But if you
have a hurried charter, you may have to just do a
hard reset and see what happens. People rarely
like standards to become more stringent. But you
know who does? A-players who are sick of watch-
ing people do less than they should.

Be careful.

High Morale, High Talent

If your evaluation reveals that your team has
high morale and is highly talented—congratula-
tions, you've hit the jackpot. It's go time.

You'll just need to prioritize getting buy-in; once you
have it, you'll be able to accomplish great things.
You can expedite this process by encouraging par-
ticipation and harnessing your people's strengths.
They'll have a lot of them, and they'll probably have
a lot of good ideas for how to use them.

Be collaborative. And grateful.

Balanced

Finally, most teams tend to fall somewhere within the gray middle area of this chart. They are emotionally okay but they have a few issues. They have an average level of talent with a few notable strengths and weaknesses.

If your team is balanced, your path forward should be more heavily impacted by the other factors in play (charter and culture). You will want to make personnel decisions in consideration of your charter, especially.

Be strategic.

THE POINT OF UNDERSTANDING YOUR TEAM

People are complicated, but the keys to decision making from a team perspective can be boiled down to talent and morale. When you know how the people you'll be leading rate on these two factors, you can determine how to lead them more effectively.

The key is to recognize that your new team may require a different leadership style than you're used to.

You likely have some sense of your leadership style; you might view yourself as a servant leader, or authoritative, or authoritarian, or democratic, or hands-off—or some other style that suits your personality and values. And that's fine. Most of us have a preferred style.

But your style needs to flex to fit your team. Too often, new executives don't meet their team where they are.

Take, for example, a CXO I worked with at a financial services company, whom I'll call Bob. He'd recently taken a new role within his organization, inheriting a new team that a colleague had spent the previous five years building. His predecessor was nothing short of beloved—but, as it turned out, not for all of the right reasons.

Bob took the position with some institutional knowledge about his new team, but only once he was leading them did he see firsthand the

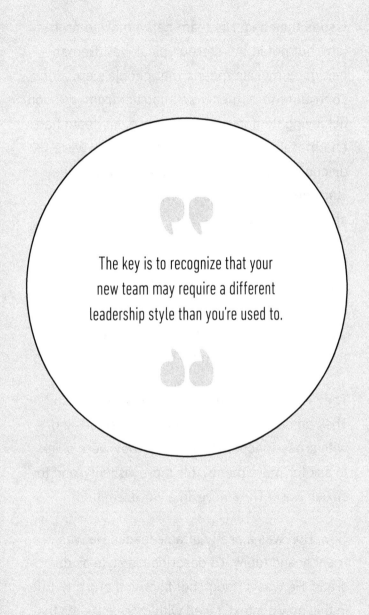

The key is to recognize that your
new team may require a different
leadership style than you're used to.

issues they had. His team had a morale problem, but not in the stereotypical way. Remember, good morale means that people's emotions contribute to, rather than subtract from, the unit achieving its goals. In Bob's case, his team had bad morale, but it wasn't because they were discouraged and overly critiqued. In fact, they were quite spoiled, and it was harming their ability to function.

Bob saw quickly that the previous leader had inflated the team's egos (and their pay scales). The team *was* very talented, but they'd been told so and treated like it too often and, over time, they'd lapsed into harmful behaviors.

They viewed themselves as "the golden group." They demonstrated low urgency when dealing with cross-functional partners. They were quick to ask for more money, for more visibility, and for sexier work. They were, in a word, entitled.

Now, Bob was a pretty affable leader. He was friendly and funny; I'd describe his style as democratic. He was a "tough but fair" kind of a guy. But in this new context, faced with morale issues that were hindering his success, he struggled to be tough enough.

I vividly recall conducting a new leader assimilation session for his team. Typically in these sessions, we gather input from the team, identify issues the team would like to solve with the leader, and then spend the rest of the day solving them. I'll never forget this group—they looked at their mobile devices the entire four hours.

Bob said nothing.

On a break, I asked their HR consultant to help me draw the team out, because they were, quite literally, phoning the session in. She agreed and told me she'd try to help get them engaged.

Then we went back in, and she said and did nothing.

I was frustrated with her, but it went beyond that; I found that leading the rest of the session made me want to chew my arm off. I'm passionate about executive assimilation, and that's the only time I remember thinking, "I can't even bring myself to care about these people."

I have to say, if that had been my team, I would have been absolutely mortified. In a situation like that, it is actually *my* job to make them put their phones down and engage, and I was so shocked at their behavior that I didn't. I felt like I had ended up in *The Twilight Zone*. After 20 years, it's hard to surprise me—but not impossible!

Bob never redirected his team. I wondered if he would address the issues the team was having; he didn't. He needed a more serious voice, a stronger voice, a more demanding voice, until their behavior stopped warranting it. Instead, he was entirely too nice, choosing to show funny YouTube videos to make people laugh and never bringing his team's attention to the issues at hand. He was as impossible to focus as they were.

It would have been wise for him to adopt, at least for a time, a more authoritative style. But Bob was intent on managing as the affable, funny leader—a style that simply wasn't appropriate with that group.

He was asked to "retire" eight months later. You can't save them all.

But you can save your chances of success if you are willing to adapt your leadership style to fit the talent and morale of your team.

The more your team is an outlier in morale or talent, the more you'll need to consider this factor as you develop your approach. Conversely, the more balanced your team is, the less heavily you'll need to weigh this factor in relation to the other two.

How to Gain Insight

How to
Gain Insight

Throughout the previous four chapters, you've read about the three critical factors in your success as a new executive. Before we move forward, let's take a moment to review what we've covered.

Here's what you should know about your new role within the first six to 12 months. Learning is iterative and ongoing, but critical mistakes within the first six months can be hard to overcome, so prioritize these discovery conversations.

Charter

Your charter is what your new organization, *cumulatively*, expects you to accomplish, and the *pace* at which they expect you to accomplish it.

You know what results are expected of you and how long you have to achieve them. Based on these two factors, you recognize the type of charter that you're facing, and therefore adapt your leadership style to that end.

Culture

The culture is the normative code of behavior in your new organization.

You grasp what behaviors are rewarded and what behaviors don't seem to be tolerated. You've begun to gauge where the new culture lies on a range of dynamic tension, and to adjust your leadership behavior to fit the norms to the extent that you can, *hopefully* without compromising your integrity.

Team

Your team is the group of people directly under your leadership.

You've assessed the morale on your team and identified the emotional and mental states that are impacting their ability to succeed. You've evaluated your team's talent and identified how capable they are of achieving the objectives defined in your charter. Based on these two factors, you recognize the type of team that you're leading, and that should influence your leadership style as well.

HOW TO GATHER THIS INFORMATION

Assessing these three factors takes time and diligence. People don't often want to deliver grim facts, or there may be political or social reasons why people may not be totally open and honest with you. But you won't be equipped to make credible decisions until you understand the perspectives of your stakeholders, so you have keep digging. If you ask enough people enough questions, you'll eventually gain an adequate picture. New executives can spend months to more than a year on this vital relationship-building and learning process.

As we've discussed in previous chapters, you'll need to meet with a broad group of stakeholders to uncover information about your charter, culture, and team. There's nuance to this. You may want to make time to periodically meet with each of your peers and direct reports one on one. Building relationships quickly is the best way to both learn and build trust. You may need to meet with more people at once via group coffees, office hours, or "town hall" meetings if you inherit a larger organization. Whatever formal structures you want to rely on, the key is to ask quality questions and listen for common themes. If there is a muscle you need to flex, it's your curiosity.

In addition to more formal settings, you should be vigilant in looking for shared spaces to have conversations. Ask people to get coffee or to grab lunch. Walk the same direction with someone after a meeting and carve out a few minutes for small talk.

(Introverts, I can hear you protesting from here. I'm introverted, too, and I hate small talk. It makes me feel socially awkward. But these casual conversations are important. Try to think of small talk as "shop talk." It helps a little.)

In all of your interactions, you should be intentional to both get to know people as individuals and let them get to know you. People will automatically be curious about you, and that's fine. But remember to stay curious about them and their insights into the work you're there to do. I recommend keeping a notebook of people's answers—*don't carry it with you*, but make sure you write things down as you learn from various sources of insight. Otherwise, you *will* forget what people communicate, and the patterns of answers are easier to recognize when they physically exist on the same page for weeks and months to come.

With your direct reports, you can be more formal. Depending on the size of your team, you may have time to meet with everyone one on one. Or you might choose to hold a listening session to get information in a collaborative setting.

QUESTIONS TO ASK

With the process clarified, here are questions I've found to be particularly revealing. (You'll recognize some of these from the previous three chapters.) The key is not to make anyone feel they are being interviewed, even as you're interviewing them. I interview thousands of executives a year and I have found a very simple formula that works: Be clear with your intent.

For example: "I'm Bob. I'm new here and I'd love to sit down and meet you and learn more about how my sales group works with your marketing group. Can you make time for that?"

Assuming you do meet with the marketing leader, ask her about herself: what she does, how long she's been with the firm, any challenges or exciting innovations her team is working on. People *love* to talk about themselves, and those are easy questions to answer. By being transparent about your intent, you diffuse most skepticism. And by starting the conversation with questions about her and her work, you naturally create opportunities to find connections between her world and yours.

Chances are also high that, during the course of the conversation, something she'll say will make it perfectly natural to ask broader questions about your team or the company as a whole. Depending on her insights you may find she knows more about the company than about your team specifically. You may find that your roles overlap, and it's never too soon to ask for feedback on how things have been going under prior leadership and to learn what might make things better for others. Most people value shared responsibility and cooperation and want to help you succeed.

Focus your questions on areas where your colleague seems to have line of sight, interest, knowledge, or common objectives. Some people will tell you everything, some will tell you a little, but most will be useful. Just make sure they know that you appreciate their insights, and keep the lines open for any future conversations that would be mutually beneficial in the future.

Ask your boss:

- What's the most important deliverable for us in the next 12 months?
- What are the biggest roadblocks you think I'll face?
- What did my predecessor do particularly well? Any troubled results I've inherited?
- What does the organization think of my team?

Ask your predecessor (if they are still around):

- What were the most important things that you've accomplished?
- What's next for this team, in your view?
- Anything you wish you had done differently?

Ask your peers:

- What have you experienced when working with my team?

- What changes are you hoping for?
  Which are most important?
- Any insights on what it's like to work for
  [insert name of boss]. Anything he/she
  clearly wants/doesn't want from their team?
- Any roadblocks between our teams that
  I should be aware of?
- How can our teams support each other?
- In the past, were roles and responsibil-
  ities between our groups clear? Are the
  handoffs good?

Ask your direct reports:

- How do you hope things change about the
  way our team works together?
- What's the hardest thing this team has
  been through?
- What's the best thing this team has
  accomplished?
- When I talk to my peers about our team's
  performance, what am I likely to hear?

- What is everyone going to miss about their old boss? Anything you won't miss? (Best used if the former boss is not still working in the company, or if your current boss was their old boss.)

Ask anyone:

- What do the most successful leaders here do differently than everyone else?
- When leaders fail here, what is usually the cause?
- If you were in my shoes, what would you be prioritizing?
- In 24 months, where do you hope we'll be?
- In five years, what do you hope we'll be doing differently? What are the audacious goals?

Any of these questions, asked of stakeholders in a variety of settings both formal and informal, should give you insight into the organization, your

team, and the broader culture. Plus, you'll learn so
much about shared history, context, and your job.

The key is to be curious.

Often, leaders—especially assimilating leaders—
use questions as an interrogation or a sort of
indictment. Don't.

Instead, be diligent, and use formal and informal
settings to weave a common set of questions
that will make sense for your stakeholders. At all
costs, avoid criticizing too much too soon. And
don't wince.

Welcome to the Trenches

Welcome to the Trenches

If you've made it this far, you're in much better shape than you were four chapters ago. You know the factors you need to be aware of to succeed in your new role. Most new executives don't. That gives you a leg up.

But it's only the beginning. To thrive in a new executive role, you have to walk the walk.

So in this section, we'll go over tactical examples of behaviors to avoid and behaviors to emulate. These insights are based on years of work with hundreds of new-to-role executives, and if you put them into practice, you'll do well. It's hard work, though, and you will face two major obstacles in implementing these tactics.

First, you're going to be scared.

You might not want to admit this. But the sooner you come to terms with it, the better you'll be able to deal with it. Most people are scared by the increased responsibility, visibility, and accountability of broader leadership. Most people have some version of imposter syndrome, a fear of failure, or of being in over their heads. It's totally normal with any big bump in pay or responsibility.

You'll be determining the fate of other people's careers. You'll be lonely, with fewer peers than your direct reports and less support (hand-holding) from above. You'll have a huge responsibility for organizational success, which means that you'll also have a huge responsibility for any failure— and, as we discussed in Chapter 2, the odds that you'll fail are significant. All of this means that if you aren't at least a little scared by the prospect of taking a new executive role, you're either so experienced that you probably don't need this book or you're a sociopath. Hopefully you aren't both.

Buckle up. Fear tends to subside after six to 12 months, but it will be your reality in the short term.

Second, as a result of your fear, you will be tempted to make decisions that are driven by your ego.

When people are scared, they don't perform at their best. Instead of acting rationally and calmly, they tend to go into flight, fight, freeze, or appease mode. Executives, in general, are more inclined toward actions that are on the fight side of that spectrum. Many new executives act rashly or bluntly assert power in an attempt to build respect quickly and assuage their own fears.

To put it simply: You're more likely to act in off-putting ways when you're new to the role.

As a new leader, you'll want to prove yourself and to assert your authority to ensure that you don't fail. But, ironically, by acting like a jerk, you'll do the opposite. If you make missteps before you build trust and get buy-in from your

So be aware of your fear.
Acknowledge it.

new team, you'll flail, isolate yourself from power, and flame out.

So be aware of your fear. Acknowledge it. Realize that it will incline you to make ego-based decisions, and consciously make an effort to saddle those inclinations. The stress you feel can drive your performance, but you need to face it first.

You can do this. In the upcoming chapters, I'll show you how.

We'll cover early missteps to avoid in Chapter 10. Then, in Chapter 11, we'll review three critical tips from the trenches to build your confidence. As with the three factors we reviewed in Chapter 8, once you know what to look for and what to avoid, you'll have a far greater chance of success.

It's time to put principles into practice. Are you ready to walk the walk?

Let's start with where you shouldn't step.

Landmines

Landmines

There are plenty of mistakes you can make as a new executive, but most of them boil down to some variation of these seven. Be diligent to avoid these missteps.

The good news is that when you know where they lie, you'll be able to change your course before they blow up your chances of success.

MISTAKE #1: HOLDING TIGHT TO THE 100-DAY PLAN.

Don't hold onto it—ditch it entirely.

This idea may be shocking, but since you've read through the previous pages, it probably isn't coming as too much of a surprise. It's simply not possible to know everything about your charter, culture, and team before you're in the role. Remember the Marshmallow Challenge from Chapter 4? Overplan and you'll end up with wreckage.

Your plan shouldn't precede your first day. So don't make one before then.

If someone asks for a plan right off the bat, tell them you'll spend 90 days listening, learning, and assessing, and 10 days circling back with stakeholders about what you have learned. They won't know what to make of that response—and that's okay. Hundred-day plans don't determine or predict success. Generating results with minimal noise does.

Instead of creating a plan, you should establish a wide web of stakeholders, as we've discussed, and meet with them to ask questions about the function you now own. Take a diagnostic approach. Be systematic and consistent in the questions you ask of all stakeholders—direct reports, peers, internal customers, external customers, boss(es).

Listen. Take notes. And build relationships. Let
people get to know you as a human. Take an
interest in who they are and what they care
about.

Then follow up with your insights and learnings.
Spend one-on-one (or small group) time with
everyone in your downline, especially if it's fewer
than 150 people. Until you can articulate the
state of affairs, important historical contexts, and
industry trends in your stakeholders' words, keep
learning.

There are exceptions to this reserved approach
that we'll address later, but in general, cool
your jets and get your assessment of priorities,
objectives, and talent right by taking time to be
thoughtful and thorough.

The team will be more open to your ideas and
agenda when they see that you've done your
homework—you understand the current business reality and why things are the way they are.
Don't mistake curiosity for weakness or poor
leadership.

MISTAKE #2: THINKING YOU HAVE A LOT TO PROVE.

This assumption is just your ego talking.

Remember, the fear of failure and the insecurity of being new can make even the most seasoned executive nervous—and those vulnerable feelings often lead to overcompensating or seeking to prove your capability.

Here's a quick list of ways you might be tempted to prove yourself that you should avoid:

- Talking too much about past accomplishments
- Talking too much about your prior firm
- Name-dropping the awesome people you've worked for in the past
- Using big words unnecessarily
- Being overly critical of the status quo and current talent
- Being arrogant, all knowing, and unrelatable

You get the picture. Most people can recognize overcompensation when they see it in others. But it's harder to spot in a mirror.

Instead of earning you the respect of your team, these behaviors create resistance. Resistance is expensive in lost synergies, lack of support, time, stress, and failure to capture any discretionary energy from those you need to move your agenda forward. You'll get enough natural resistance from people; you shouldn't manufacture more with these poor behaviors.

In other words, don't behave like Valia.

Valia was a hire at the university where I worked years ago, before I was in the executive assimilation space at all. She was brought in because her husband had taken the Vice Chancellor position at our campus. The school had a generous "trailing spouse" policy, which meant that whenever a spouse took a tenured role at the university, we often created positions for their spouse as well. As you can imagine, there are only so many jobs in any market for a PhD in economics, so creating space for a trailing spouse was in theory a good talent-attraction strategy.

Valia was given the responsibility of running a program assessment in my home department.

At our university, these assessments happened every seven years, and they covered everything the department was doing, from the coursework, to the success rates of past students, to alumni wages, you name it. We then built plans to improve any weaknesses that the assessment revealed.

On paper, Valia was well-suited for this role because she'd run program assessments at a smaller university in the past.

In reality, she was a nightmare.

I vividly remember our first meeting. We were sitting in a room for a facilitated session with all of the full-time faculty, with the goal of reviewing our past seven years' worth of work and creating the yearlong plan for assessment. Valia led us through the standard assessment questions and our faculty responded with their answers based on the work they'd done.

Valia's reactions to our answers made it clear that she thought we were imbeciles.

"Really?" she'd say, seemingly in disbelief. "You're still doing things that way? *Wow.*"

Then, she'd inhale sharply between her clenched teeth, shake her head gravely, wince, and say, "Ummmmmm. Okay?" It was obvious that, in her opinion, she was incredibly smart, and our department had wasted most of a decade with our utter ineptitude.

(Mind you, she came from a university that was your basic Walmart, and we were solidly Target+. It was probably not the right tone for the meeting. Now, if she'd come from Harvard, maybe we would have been starstruck and overlooked her patronization.)

I now believe that Valia was trying to prove herself—to solidify her position by demonstrating her own competence, loudly. She couldn't talk enough about better approaches; she couldn't say more to belittle our status quo. She seemed to enjoy ending controversial departmental meetings with, "Well, let's just remember who is sleeping with your boss, shall we?" (I wish I was making that up, but I am not.) People will broker power in the most

MISTAKE #4: FEELING THE PRESSURE TO DRIVE A UNIQUE VISION AND AGENDA.

It's less about *your* agenda and more about *shared* vision.

Ideally, visions are shaped by teams, not by one powerful voice. You might be the smartest person in the room (although I hope you haven't tried overly hard to prove it). But if you want buy-in from the people who will make or break your results through their execution, you'll need to include their perspectives.

Instead of trying to impose your own agenda, you should collaboratively establish a roadmap and priorities with the people who will be responsible for delivering them. You can push, pull, and exert your influence, but your people have to have some real measure of impact on the vision, too. You're new-to-role, which means that your people will have more firsthand knowledge of how things work, more history with what doesn't, and maybe even more subject-matter expertise.

fascinating ways. Businesses and people do so much better without this dysfunctional posturing.

As you might expect, her attempt to appear smart created resistance. Within three years she had exhausted any support she once enjoyed and an exit was the only solution left for her. Fortunately her husband got a better job, and she followed him on his tailcoats once more.

Here's the takeaway: Stop trying to prove you're the smartest person in the room. In the long run, results will prove your efficacy and your worth as a leader, not your ability to sound impressive. You may feel that asking questions or not having the answers will make you seem weak, but it won't. It will make you seem real. You can reduce resistance when you prove less and listen more.

Instead of acting like Valia, let your people know that you are there to learn, observe, and understand the history and context of your new assignment. Don't flaunt your opinions about how things are until you can articulate your department's state of affairs as well as someone who has been there for a few years. Share only what seems relevant about your past, and show respect to legacy employees and their contributions, even if their methods seem archaic.

The way things are in your new role is the result of their work—their hard work. Do not call their baby ugly. You can't help being an outsider, but you *can* reserve judgment for a little while.

When you have done your due diligence, your answers and ideas will have appropriate context. Your opinion will be grounded, your future vision will be credible, and your contributions will incorporate stakeholder input in a way that's appealing.

As you build relationships and influence, you'll gain a stronger foundation for making decisions and inciting change.

MISTAKE #3: STRIVING TO APPEAR DECISIVE ON TALENT.

Putting the business ahead of your people will not get the results you're looking for in the long term. It may not even get results in the short term.

It's true that coming in and being decisive is important in some contexts. However, unless you're tasked with a turnaround, you have time to be thoughtful about your people. Take it. Be patient as you assess, repurpose, coach, or manage someone out (if you must).

Remember Roy's approach? Give your people a chance. By doing the most that you can to salvage existing talent without hindering results, you'll earn grace with people you lead. And you really need their trust.

If you're too quick to move out existing talent and bring in your own people, you'll risk alienating your remaining direct reports and their peers, all of whom you need to align with.

Your team will understand that not everyone will make the cut—and, ultimately, they won't respect you if tolerate poor performance indefinitely. But grace is the best approach. If your team sees you trying to make the best of it while balancing the business result, you will not unnecessarily alienate anyone.

On top of it all, they have to do the work—so let them help build what's next. People who buy in will give more discretionary effort, work with more integrity, cooperate more readily, and boost team morale.

All of this mitigates resistance that can (and does) slow results in tangible and intangible ways.

MISTAKE #5: TRYING TO "ALWAYS KEEP 'EM GUESSING."

Please don't do this.

Being unclear can seem appealing as a power play; it might also be a way to opt out of making tough decisions. But the reality is that letting roles, responsibilities, accountabilities, communication cadences, expectations, and your hot button issues remain a mystery is irresponsible and cruel—plus, it's ineffective.

For example, I had an engagement with a firm that brought in a new CFO named Chris. He was coming from GE, where the culture is aggressive and bombastic, and he was stepping into an organization that was gentle and people-driven, so I had a worry bubble about him from the start.

My firm didn't support Chris' assimilation, but we did support people that reported to him. Honestly, I've never seen someone create as much fear in as short a time as he did.

Chris was the definition of a boss who keeps people guessing. To begin, he set no expectations on how he wanted people to communicate with him; in fact, quite the opposite. His reports would come to meetings with no idea of what to expect and no idea of how to prepare—and then, in those meetings, Chris would light them up, criticize them, and shut them down in 10 minutes. They'd leave looking for answers and trying to figure out who was doing well.

Not many were. Chris terrified his people.

It was actually rather impressive, because his team was made up of smart folks with tons of education who were making millions of dollars a year. But Chris was just on a power trip; he didn't generate results.

Chris did zero outreach, didn't take time to get to know people, and didn't include anybody in his vision. As a result, nobody was on the bus for it. The department became a stressful place to work, and the energy that Chris's team spent trying to figure him out could have been spent on actual work.

Chris is still in his seat, but his department has lost some really good, essential leaders and is struggling. It's hardly surprising. The irony is that people who don't think they need help assimilating into a role usually need it the most. Hubris is dangerous.

The takeaway is that you can have high standards— but you have to communicate what they are.

The people you lead *want* to make you happy and
want to avoid getting on your bad side; those are
the things that matter for *their* success. So make
it easy for them to succeed, and let them know
what your expectations are. Don't make your
team resort to reading the tea leaves or experi-
encing your leadership style through trial by fire.

You should strive for clarity and transparency.
Clarity is more humane—and more effective—
than guessing games. If all your team knows
about dealing with you is to "be brilliant, be brief,
and be gone!" you've done a poor job of helping
them to calibrate to you. Be explicit. Have expec-
tation-setting conversations early in your tenure,
meaning within three months of taking your seat.

If you are transparent, you'll enable your team to
stop focusing on unraveling the mystery of you
and get back to focusing on what you really want:
delivering results.

MISTAKE #6: HOLDING ONTO BAD NEWS FOR TOO LONG.

Bad news ages poorly. Delivering it honestly and quickly is the best approach.

And yet, when faced with bad news—a mistake or a missed goal—many new executives try to mask the truth. They may hide details, or try to buy time to course correct before the boss or other powerful stakeholders find out.

Why?

As we've covered, it's often because they're scared.

It's easy to feel pressure to look like you're "getting it." It's intimidating to be faced with results you probably won't hit. And it's human nature to want to look good to others.

But there are two encouraging truths you need to keep in mind when you're faced with a decision to share bad news or sit on it.

First, unless you're in a very harsh culture, people accept that others (even executives) have a learning curve.

They expect progress, not perfection. That's partly because change is now considered constant, and with change comes some risk of failure and lessons learned. Consequently, most people watch for the pattern of learning, the pattern of decision-making, and the pattern of results—not the minutiae of their new executive's every move.

Second, with few exceptions, vulnerability yields trust.

When leaders bring forth problems with openness and transparency in a timely manner, most people will lean in and help, even the boss. Few will take that vulnerability and stab it through the heart. (Some will, but I promise you, you really don't want to work for those people.)

So if you make a mistake or if results aren't what you were hoping to achieve, be honest.

Because if you're not—if you allow issues to fester until they're too obvious to be ignored—you're going to be treated much less generously. Your upline leaders will lose more trust in you than if you'd simply presented the situation quickly. You could be fired.

Bad news goes down more easily and with less resistance when it's still news. No one appreciates a cover up.

MISTAKE #7: BRINGING IN "YOUR GUYS."

You may be tempted to bring along old colleagues as you enter a new position. Maybe you want some support right off the bat, or maybe you review your team and decide that better talent is needed.

Great—it's okay to bring in previous colleagues. It's not okay to bring in "your guys."

For example, I worked with an executive named Doug who brought in Rob, a previous coworker, to help head up his new team. Off the bat, this didn't look great; the company had been focusing on hiring females for leadership roles and Doug had hired a man without going through much of a process.

Still, things could have worked out, except for the fact that Rob was "Doug's guy."

Every time Doug and Rob interacted, they made references to their past work. Every time Doug had an opinion, Rob agreed with him. To make matters worse, Doug and Rob looked like they could have been brothers.

Doug's new team noticed all of this. They didn't like it.

The team felt disrespected by Doug and resentful toward Rob, and, as a result, their collaboration was sabotaged. The department developed an "us-versus-them" mentality that undermined its ability to function. Unsurprisingly, Doug and Rob didn't last very long.

If you want to bring in a previous colleague (or even colleagues), you can. But, to make things work, you need to carefully avoid making this person "your guy." This means that you should not constantly reference your past work or shared social connections. You should be upfront with your new team and tell them that you've worked with the person before, but you should emphasize your colleague's fit on your current team rather than your shared past.

For example: "Lauren will be a great fit here. I know she's great at X, so she'll be helpful as we pursue this initiative." Then, never talk about your previous connection in front of your team again.

Additionally, it's best when hires from previous roles don't agree with everything you say and think. In fact, they should look for opportunities to disagree with you. The more they offer their own perspectives, the clearer it will become that they're their own person, not "your guy."

And, finally, fair warning: Hiring someone who looks like they could be your sibling can be a risky move.

Pressure-Tested Advice

Pressure-Tested Advice

We've covered the land mines you need to avoid. Now, let's talk through the tactics you need to deploy.

The following stems from years of experience in executive assimilation. Take these tips to heart and you'll gain a more accurate perspective and the confidence you need to succeed.

TIP #1: YOU'RE NOT IN THIS ALONE.

Executive roles can feel lonely. You face pressing demands and have fewer peers to confide in. It can feel like the weight of the world is on your shoulders.

You aren't in it alone.

But don't let the position fool you: You aren't in it alone. If you want to succeed, you have to view your charter as an "us" thing.

This is why you can't afford to alienate stakeholders early in your new role. You need them because the only way you can accomplish your objectives is through their good work. And believe it or not, they need you to need them, too. Being useful feels good. Your people want to be empowered and may even want a chance to play the hero by coming to the rescue. If you insist on playing the lone wolf in your new role, you'll deny your people what they want and need most.

Don't.

Instead, ask for their help. Nothing conveys "I'm in this with you" more effectively than asking for input. Put your pride down. If you're a male, put it down twice. Empower your subject-matter experts. Seek input. Find allies. Build mutual trust and shared objectives.

Because the only way you'll win is if your team wins.

TIP #2: THEY GOT THE HIRE RIGHT.

When I took on the work of executive assimilation, my biggest concern was that my clients would pair me with an executive who was a terrible fit for the role, then put me on the hook for their success.

I have good news, though, for you and for me: Most often, higher-ups tend to put the right butt in the right executive seat.

Once in a while, as I start working with an executive, I'll think, "Wow, what were the higher-ups thinking? This person is *way* off for this role."

It happens. And yet, my firm has a 98% assimilation success rate. Even when new executives don't fit well at all, we've still helped them thrive.

How?

Through strategy. Because having a smart plan for stepping into a role outweighs being a perfect fit for that role.

The truth is that people that are supposedly perfect fits for their roles fail, too—half of the time,
actually. So take confidence in the fact that smart
people put you in your role, and trust their judgment. There's no such thing as a perfect fit, and
being strategic is a better early indicator of a successful appointment, anyway.

TIP #3: SET A PURPOSE BEYOND YOURSELF.

Coaching executives to assimilate has taught
me a lot about fear- and ego-driven behaviors.
Here's what I've seen, again and again: The executives that care only about themselves are the
executives who are most afraid to fail.

That's because the desire to prove yourself is a
negative desire; it's a desire to *avoid* negative per-
ception, and it only leads inward, toward fear.

Fear hurts performance. People do not think cre-
atively, strategically, or clearly when they are acting in fear. There's nothing strategic about fight,

flight, freeze, or appease. Those are reactions, not intentional behaviors. Fear is effective in the jungle, but not so much in the boardroom.

This plays out in your interactions with people, in your decision-making processes, and in the day-to-day functions of your role.

I saw this play out for Arthur, who was hired to do a turnaround.

Shortly after he took his position, his function faced some regulatory challenges; it wasn't his fault, but the person before him had done something that federal authorities didn't like, and so Arthur was left to deal with a tricky situation. On top of that, he was a newly promoted VP in a department that had been underperforming for years. And on top of *that*, he was the sole provider for his family.

He had the world on his shoulders. He was stressed and scared—and his fear impacted his business relationships.

Arthur was in a function where hiring and promoting diversity was viewed as a critical initiative,
and his closest peer—who was also a new VP and
high-achiever—was female.

Arthur's fear made him cautious to engage with
her. He couldn't help thinking, "If she's the hotshot
with all the potential and she's a woman, is that
going to reduce my chances for promotion?"

Because he was scared of being outperformed,
his initial instinct was to withhold information
from her—to keep her out of the loop so that
she wouldn't look very good. Author sounds like
a jerk, but he wasn't. This is the power fear has
over our leadership behaviors.

When people are afraid, they're more likely to be
competitive than cooperative, often to the detri-
ment of the firm.

Fortunately, in our discussions, we were able to
navigate his fear. We visualized what it would look
like to cut his peer off and, on the flipside, what
it would look like to help his colleague. Arthur
came to a vision where he could be extremely

cooperative and helpful. He ended up working really well with his fellow VP, and the story ended happily; he got promoted to a different part of the company and she left. He could have done a lot of damage by withholding information, but he set an intention to help. To be the sort of colleague who helped women advance.

And that's the key: A goal beyond yourself is a positive desire. It's a desire to *achieve* something for others, *with* others, and it gives you a path forward.

So instead of acting in fear and trying to prove yourself, try to achieve a higher good for your organization. This might be its mission, its customer experience, or your people's advancement—but it must be a purpose beyond yourself. Take the time to clarify this early in your new role.

As you do so, be real, be transparent, and be open to collaboration. Share information. If the environment is so bad that you can't avoid the toxicity of fear, you should probably get out of the seat before you are poisoned by it.

Your purpose can't be to prove your worth. If it is, you won't be worth much.

TIP #4: BE KIND.

This sounds trite, I know. But in today's world, where we live with a social media culture of total transparency and an internet that never forgets, being thoughtful of how you treat other humans has become a critical competency.

Believe it or not, being nice wasn't always essential, at least in the same way it is today.

That's not because people used to enjoy working for jerks; it's because, in the dark ages, it was far harder to tell if someone was a jerk. No one got 360° feedback, engagement scores weren't a thing, and Glassdoor didn't exist. So if you got results by being a jerk, your boss may not have known and, even if they did, they probably wouldn't have cared, as long as you boosted the bottom line.

Now, organizations have to care. Executive-ready talent is harder to come by, transparency is heightened, and technology means anyone can know anything about you in three clicks. And one thing that hasn't changed is that no one wants to work for a jerk.

Look: You're a human. Leading humans. Who have lives and problems and talents and shortcomings. As do you.

Be thoughtful of them. If you're kind to your people, and if you support them when and where you can, and if you do your best to consider and meet their needs, then they will take care of you tenfold. Legitimate kindness is nearly always reciprocated.

This is the most under-leveraged business concept on the planet. Make it your secret weapon.

Kindness and thoughtfulness do *not* dilute high standards. If you are fair and kind, you have every right to maintain high standards and people will work hard to meet them.

TIP #5: ATTRACT THE BEST TALENT.

Attract the best talent and you'll be far more likely to succeed. Repel talent and you'll probably fail.

This flows naturally from being kind, but that's only the starting point. Here's the key: To attract and retain the best talent (after you've done your initial assessment and rejiggering of the team), you will need to create a culture that A-players can thrive in.

Whether you call them rock stars, high performers, or just awesome employees, these are the people you should seek to build your new team around—and that means you must build things in a way that appeals to them.

A-players want autonomy. They want a voice. They want recognition, challenge, and visibility. They want to be given stretch goals and development opportunities. They want to learn and they want to grow.

In short, they want to be maximized.

So, create an environment where they can be. You'll need to make accountabilities clear; give your people explicit goals to hit and hold a very high bar for yourself and for them. Provide appropriate air cover and feedback—be there when they need you and then get out of the way.

Pete was an SVP who did this exceptionally well. He was charismatic, tall, with executive presence for days. Perhaps that *shouldn't* have anything to do with attracting A-players, but hey, it helps.

He came from a sales background, so he was social and charming—he was phenomenal in "town hall" meetings. Most important, he was adept at keeping the noise in his organization quiet while simultaneously knowing how to push people.

He excelled at identifying talent and promoting the people who were probably going to be successful but who didn't easily believe in themselves. He breathed life into them; under Pete's watch, there were plenty of stories that went something like, "I'm the first college grad in my family, and now I'm a Fortune 500 executive." He had an eye.

Over time, that earned Pete the reputation that he cared about talent management and that he got people promoted based on merit. He was always there to help people figure it out, but he also gave a lot of latitude.

As a result, Pete has a brand that has moved around with him over the course of his career. People follow him. He's honest, fair, upholds high standards, and gives freedom, autonomy, visibility. A-players want to work for him, because A-players thrive on bosses like Pete.

If *you* do these things, you can turn a function that can't attract talent into a "destination function" that A-players actively seek out.

And if A-players are actively seeking you out, you'll start hitting your goals. Fast.

"She who has the best talent wins." Never forget that.

Conclusion

Conclusion

Amara

"What the hell did I get myself into?"

That was Roy's question years ago as we sat down to talk about his seemingly overwhelming position. As you began to read this book, I'm guessing it was your question, too. I hope that you now have an answer. And I also hope that, just as Roy came to enjoy his position as he implemented a strategic approach, you come to find your role enjoyable, too.

Because, while there's no debating that you've gotten yourself into a challenging spot by taking a new executive role, the good news is that you have a high chance of succeeding if you put into practice all that we've covered over the previous pages. And the best news of all is that by leading well you can make a difference—in your organization and in your own life.

The approach I've spelled out in this book is simple in concept but can be difficult in application. It boils down to three things:

Take the time to understand your charter, your team, and your culture. Don't act in fear. And please don't be a jerk.

As you get back to the trenches, I want to leave you with a final example to follow: Be like Amara.

I worked with Amara at a mid-sized finance institution. She'd just stepped up from leading a small team to leading a large team, which meant she'd also stepped up into much more scrutiny and pressure. She was anxious, as anyone would be—as you might be right now.

The pressure on Amara wasn't immediate; her organization's charter wasn't urgent and there wasn't a high degree of change expected from her. But the bad news was that she worked for a difficult boss who was quick to push back on ideas, especially if those ideas didn't yield immediate results.

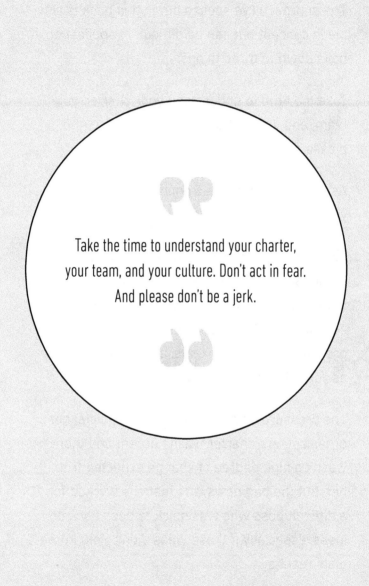

Take the time to understand your charter, your team, and your culture. Don't act in fear. And please don't be a jerk.

Yet Amara was committed to learning in her new role and she spent the most time gathering feedback out of any leader I've worked with. Really—she was extreme in her willingness to meet people in her organization, and by "extreme" I mean that she committed to meeting and talking with all 400 people in the organization she was now leading.

Some people have trouble finding time for a coffee date. Finding time for hundreds of coffee dates is a huge commitment.

But Amara's efforts paid off. She started by talking with her peers and direct reports, and from there she worked slowly and methodically through every single human in her organization. Her boss, unsurprisingly, gave her a little bit of grief about how slowly she was moving, especially in the beginning. But Amara was able to articulate the value of her approach and, over time, that value took the form of tangible results.

She built connections. She heard people. She let people get to know her. Perhaps most impressive of all, she was disciplined in returning to debrief

with people: "Here's what I've heard, here's what
I've learned, here's what we'll do going forward."

Amara was extreme in her diligence and, as a
result, she experienced almost no resistance.
One person on her team grumbled because
they weren't promoted. Everyone else came to
regard Amara highly. And here's the surprise that,
by now, isn't really a surprise: She got results
quickly. Because she was respected and had
taken (a seemingly copious amount of) time to
inform her ideas through collaboration, when
she finally moved, she did so like a warm knife
through soft butter.

Even her boss was impressed.

The moral of the story? This stuff works, even if it
seems counterintuitive. Amara got results by following these tactics. You can, too.

Now, get out there, lead your people, and be
bombproof.

Good luck.

Ready to see if executive coaching is the right next step?

www.bermesassociates.com